THE WARS OF THE ROSES

A ROYAL HISTORY OF ENGLAND

THE WARS OF THE ROSES

BY ANTHONY CHEETHAM

EDITED BY
ANTONIA FRASER

University of California Press
Berkeley Los Angeles

University of California Press
Berkeley and Los Angeles, California

Published by arrangement with Cassell & Co

The text of *The Wars of the Roses* is taken from the single-volume
The Lives of the Kings & Queens of England, first published in the United Kingdom
in 1975 by Weidenfeld & Nicolson, revised in 1993 and 1998.

Text copyright © Cassell & Co 2000
Design and layout copyright © Cassell & Co 2000

Cataloging-in-Publication data is on file with the Library of Congress.

ISBN 0-520-22802-2

Jacket images: front © The Bridgeman Art Library, London (the Neville family at
prayer, by the Master of the Golden Legend in Munich, from the Neville Book of
Hours); back © The Bridgeman Art Library, London (the battle of Barnet, 1470).

Endpapers: Depiction of the seige of Calais. *Page 2*: Miniature showing a new knight of
the Bath riding through the Tower of London to present himself to Richard III.

Printed and bound in Italy.
9 8 7 6 5 4 3 2 1

CONTENTS

INTRODUCTION

The period known as the Wars of the Roses takes its name from the battle between the Houses of Lancaster and York: the red rose being the emblem of the House of Lancaster, the white the House of York. In 1399, Henry Bolingbroke, Earl of Derby and the son of John of Gaunt, seized the crown from his cousin Richard II seeking vengeance for his banishment and the loss of his inheritance rights. Once Henry had successfully dethroned Richard, the fourteen ensuing years of his kingship were troubled.

Shakespeare's plays would famously suggest that Henry IV suffered divine retribution for his usurpation of the hereditary principle. Henry IV's reign was studded by revolts and uprisings by rebel barons but, nevertheless, when he died in 1413, he passed on his country intact to his son, Prince Henry, and thereby successfully engendered a new dynasty. The coronation and reign of Henry IV had irrevocably proved, though, that the rightful royal line was precarious and that it could indeed be successfully challenged by a magnate.

Prince Hal – Henry V, Shakespeare's martial king – occupies a central position in the English historical imagination. Crowned in 1413, 'warlike Harry' is remembered for that boon companion of his youth, Falstaff, the rivalry with Hotspur, and his renowned victory at Agincourt in 1415. Henry V also epitomises the nature of medieval history and kingship: within the climate of his times, the essential skill at arms of a young knight was to be directed towards the glorification of the royal sphere of influence and the determined pursuit of any rights not yet pressed home.

In true contrast is the tragic reign of Henry V's son, Henry VI. Announced King of England before he was a year old in 1422, in 1431 Henry was also crowned King of France (making him the first sovereign of both England and France). But the situation in France was in decline and Henry's reputation suffered. Indeed, he is often remembered as irresponsible, unkingly and foolish, despite his saintlike devotion to

God and the Church. His marriage to Margaret of Anjou paradoxically resulted in the loss of land in France. Unlike his father, he lacked the regal attributes the times demanded. His reign was beset by the power struggle over succession. There was no heir until 1453 and the Dukes of York and Somerset both had an eye on the throne. It was essentially the conflict between these two dukes that sparked the Wars of the Roses.

The 'sun' of the Duke of York, Edward, was to take the English throne twice by force, but twice was defeated and forced to flee the country in humiliation. His claim to the throne lay in his descent from the second son of Edward III, whereas Henry VI was descended from John of Gaunt, the third son of Edward III. In medieval times, a monarch was expected to both look and act the part of a hero, to be both a warrior and a ruler.

Edward IV was of heroic physical stature and was described as 'the handsomest knight in England', but he did not foresee the predatory behaviour of his brother, Richard, Duke of Gloucester. When Edward IV died in 1483, Richard was appointed Protector over the King's twelve-year-old heir, Edward V, but he himself became King later in the same year.

Richard III has become one of history's villains and England's most controversial king of all. After five hundred years, the exact truth about the deaths of the young Princes in the Tower is still not known but the event has tended to overshadow the entire history of Richard III's reign. He may have been the physical antithesis of his tall, golden-haired brother, but Richard was hard-working, brave and disapproving of Edward IV's free and indulgent court lifestyle.

The usurpation of the throne, which, received opinion has it, was motivated by an unreflecting desire for power, has to be seen in the context of Richard's position in the complex family tree of York and Lancaster; and in the light of the trouble that a child king can bring to a nation.

THE HOUSES OF LANCASTER AND YORK

Showing their descent from Edward III and the Tudor claim to the throne

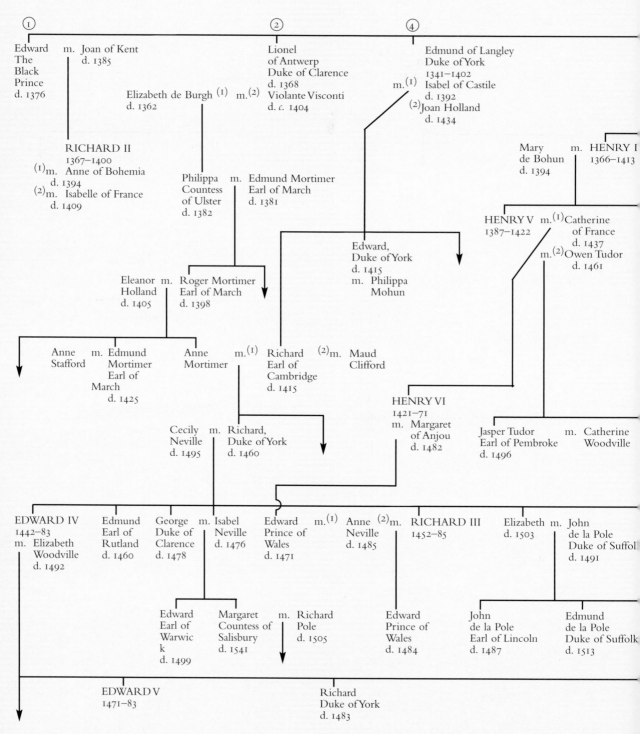

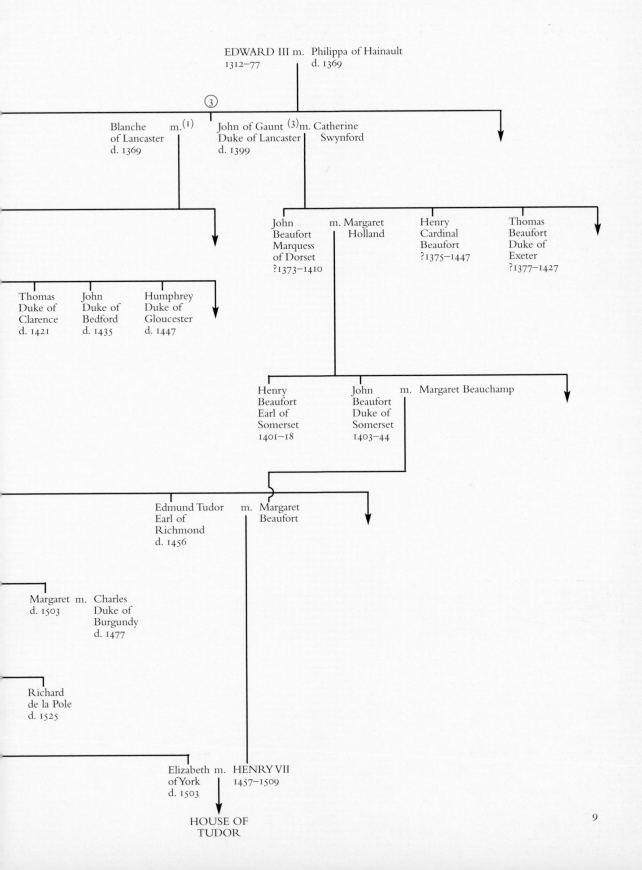

EDWARD III m. Philippa of Hainault
1312–77   d. 1369

③

Blanche   m.(1)   John of Gaunt (3)m. Catherine
of Lancaster   Duke of Lancaster   Swynford
d. 1369   d. 1399

John   m. Margaret   Henry   Thomas
Beaufort   Holland   Cardinal   Beaufort
Marquess   Beaufort   Duke of
of Dorset   ?1375–1447   Exeter
?1373–1410   ?1377–1427

Thomas   John   Humphrey
Duke of   Duke of   Duke of
Clarence   Bedford   Gloucester
d. 1421   d. 1435   d. 1447

Henry   John   m. Margaret Beauchamp
Beaufort   Beaufort
Earl of   Duke of
Somerset   Somerset
1401–18   1403–44

Edmund Tudor   m.   Margaret
Earl of   Beaufort
Richmond
d. 1456

Margaret m. Charles
d. 1503   Duke of
              Burgundy
              d. 1477

Richard
de la Pole
d. 1525

Elizabeth m. HENRY VII
of York   1457–1509
d. 1503

HOUSE OF
TUDOR

9

THE ROYAL ARMS IN THE FIFTEENTH CENTURY

IT IS SAID THAT IN 1376 CHARLES V OF FRANCE formally altered the royal arms of France by reducing the number of fleurs-de-lys to three. Various theories have been put forward as to why he did this. The most romantic is that in 496 Queen Clothilde was given a holy cloth embroidered with three lilies, symbolising the Blessed Virgin, and that she gave this cloth to her husband King Clovis. It is suggested that Charles adopted the three fleurs-de-lys in order to give official sanction to this popular legend.

Whatever reason and at what exact moment it happened, from the end of the fourteenth century the French royal arms contained but three lilies and, when a new great seal was struck for Henry IV in 1405, he followed the French King's lead and reduced the number of lilies in the French quarterings in his arms to three.

Henry V, Henry VI, Edward IV, Edward V and Richard III used more or less the same arms. The only small difference occurred in the detail of the crest. Basically it remained the same but minor variations are to be found. For example, Edward IV at one time used an uncrowned lion standing within a crown on a chapeau, as illustrated, whilst in his third great seal the crown is shown with arches. Eventually, with Henry VIII, the chapeau and coronet gave way to an arched crown and the lion was similarly crowned. This is essentially the crest of England as borne by the Queen today.

Towards the close of the fifteenth century, representations of the royal arms are found, although not on the great seal, with supporters on either side of the shield. These supporters seem to have their origin in artistry. Seal engravers, sculptors and wood carvers took the liberty of adding favourite beasts or badges to representations of arms so as to obtain a more interesting artistic effect. This custom must have pleased the nobility and more and more of them began to affect these adornments to their arms. The Kings were no exception and there are examples of the arms of Henry VI, Edward IV and Richard III supported by a variety of beasts chosen from their family, rather than their royal, heraldry.

It was not long before the heralds began to take official notice of supporters and, as it were, admit them to the field of official heraldry, recording them, assigning them and making rules for their depiction and devolution.

THE HOUSE OF LANCASTER

1399–1471

HENRY IV 1399–1413
HENRY V 1413–22
HENRY VI 1422–71

Opposite: Henry Bolingbroke (Henry v) enters London to
take the throne from Richard ii, from Jean Froissart's *Chroniques
de France et d'Angleterre.*

HENRY IV *r.* 1399-1413

IN SHAKESPEARE'S PLAYS HENRY IV is a king condemned to a sterile reign, beset by rebellious barons and an ailing body, punished by divine retribution for his usurpation of Richard's throne. This view is not far off the mark. The King who ruled England and Aquitaine for thirteen troubled years from 1399 to 1413 was a sad contrast to the brilliant, energetic and chivalrous figure of Henry Bolingbroke, Earl of Derby.

Henry was born in April 1366 at Bolingbroke Castle in Lincolnshire, the only son of John of Gaunt and his first wife, Blanche of Lancaster, to survive infancy. His parents were cousins: John was the third surviving son of Edward III and Blanche was the great-great-granddaughter of Henry III. She brought to her husband the vast estates and ducal title of Lancaster, as well as the earldoms of Derby, Lincoln and Leicester. It was in Blanche's memory that Chaucer wrote his *Book of the Duchesse*. She died in her early twenties when Henry was only three.

With his mother dead and his father usually absent on affairs of state, Henry's upbringing was entrusted largely to a group of Lancastrian retainers, some of whom remained his most trusted servants when he became King. He proved himself an able pupil, well equipped to fulfil the ideals of chivalry. With his stocky build and vigorous health he excelled at the martial arts; he was also devout, well read, a pleasant talker and an accomplished musician. Since he was so clearly destined to play an important role in the affairs of state, Henry was not permitted the obscurity of childhood. When Edward III died in 1377, he bore the sword of mercy at the coronation of his young cousin, Richard II, and was afterwards styled Earl of Derby. Three years later, at the age of fourteen, he was married to Mary de Bohun,

co-heiress of the late Earl of Hereford and Essex, a match which cost his father 5,000 marks. Mary bore him four sons and two daughters, the first being the future Henry v, who was born at Monmouth in 1387; the last was Philippa, whose birth in 1394 brought about her mother's death. Like Henry's own mother, Mary was in her early twenties when she died.

In the year which saw the birth of his first son, Henry also made his precocious entry into the political arena. By joining his name to the cause of the Lords Appellant in their semi-treasonable enterprise to

Richard II abdicates and Henry IV is proclaimed King of England in Westminster in September 1399.

unseat the King's closest counsellors, and by taking arms to block the crossing of the Thames at Radcot Bridge to Richard's special favourite, Robert de Vere, Henry sowed in his royal cousin's mind the mistrust and the thirst for vengeance which was to cost Richard his Crown and his life. Indeed there is some evidence that the Appellants meant to depose Richard after Radcot Bridge, but changed their minds when they failed to agree whether Henry or his uncle, Thomas, Duke of Gloucester, should replace him. Instead the Appellants concentrated on the persecution of Richard's servants at the Merciless Parliament of 1388. Here Henry showed a more generous spirit than his fellows by speaking up for at least one of the luckless victims, Sir Simon Burley.

Henry's initiative cannot have pleased his father, who remained until his death a faithful servant of the Crown, and it would never have taken place unless Gaunt had been absent in Spain, pressing his claim to the throne of Castile. When Gaunt returned to England late the following year (1389) his son retired to the wings and occupied himself for a while with the administration of his estates. But the conventional life of an itinerant nobleman could not contain his energies for long, and the autumn of 1390 saw Henry in command of a privately mounted expedition – part adventure, part crusade – to distant Lithuania, where he fought side by side with the Teutonic Knights at the siege of Vilna. The campaign was not arduous – Henry's band of two hundred lost only one knight killed and two captured before returning to Königsberg for Christmas, and he was accompanied throughout by a band of six minstrels. All embarked safely for England in the spring of 1391. In 1392 Henry undertook a more ambitious journey to Jerusalem, travelling overland through Frankfurt (Oder), Prague, Vienna and Venice, and then by ship to Jaffa by way of Corfu and Rhodes. On the return journey he visited Cyprus, Rhodes, Venice, Milan and Paris. This grand tour occupied nearly a year and gave Henry the opportunity to enjoy the hospitality of King Wenceslas of Bohemia, Duke Albert of Austria, the Doge of Venice, the Grand Master of the Knights Hospitaller of St John, King James I of Cyprus (who presented him with a leopard) and the Visconti Duke of Milan. Along the road he impressed his hosts with his handsome appearance, his courtesy and his fluency in English, French and Latin. Now at the age of twenty-seven he could boast the European reputation of a seasoned warrior and courtier.

The five years between Henry's return from Jerusalem and his banishment in 1398 gave little scope for the exercise of those talents. There are signs that he grew restive, for in 1396 it was said that his father forbade him to accept an invitation from William of Hainault, a distant cousin, to join him in a campaign against Friesland. More serious is the story – admittedly unsubstantiated – that Henry was party to the conspiracy, concocted by Gloucester, Arundel and Warwick in July 1397, to imprison both Gaunt and the King for life. Whatever the facts about Henry's complicity, he stood by the King when the three former Appellants were subsequently convicted of treason in Parliament, and shortly afterwards, in September 1397, he was created Duke of Hereford. The motives behind the events which followed are equally obscure. Henry's own account is that Thomas Mowbray (Earl of Nottingham and Duke of Norfolk), the man who apprised King Richard of the conspiracy, told Henry that the two of them were marked men, whom the King would bring down just as he had already brought down the other three Appellants. Mowbray apparently went on to reveal another conspiracy aimed at eliminating all the barons close to the King, including Gaunt and Henry himself. Henry then reported the conversation to his father, who in turn repeated everything to the King. In February 1398 Henry accused Mowbray of treason to his face in the King's presence: in April a court of chivalry at Windsor ordained that the two Dukes should resolve their dispute in a trial by battle, to take place at Coventry in September.

The contest never took place, for Richard decided at the last moment to banish both parties, Henry for ten years, Mowbray for life. Although Henry's sentence was subsequently reduced to six years, he now had ample reason for believing Mowbray's warning that the King meant to undo him. Nevertheless, while Gaunt lived he had no choice but to go. In Paris he was warmly greeted as one of royal rank and resided at the Hôtel Clisson. Henry had only been there for four months when he heard the news, in February 1399, of his father's death. It was then that Richard made his literally fatal mistake of altering Henry's sentence to perpetual banishment and declaring all the possessions of the House of Lancaster forfeit to the crown.

This decision opened Henry's path to the throne. No man could feel safe when the laws of inheritance could be so arbitrarily flouted, and the lifelong service of the father so shoddily repaid in the punishment of the son. Henry's prospects were enhanced by two other recent demises: that of his uncle Gloucester who had reputedly fancied himself as Richard's replacement in 1387 and again in 1397; and that of Roger

Mortimer, Earl of March, whom the childless King had recognised as his heir. Mortimer's heir was a seven-year-old boy, Edmund.

When Richard compounded his error by leaving on a punitive expedition to Ireland at such a critical juncture (May 1399), Henry gathered his followers and struck. Early in July three small ships bore him and perhaps three hundred men to Ravenspur in Yorkshire. His progress to Pontefract was more of a triumph than a campaign, for he met no opposition, and while the Duke of York, Richard's ineffectual uncle and Viceroy, dithered in the south, Henry's ranks grew with Lancastrian retainers and, more significantly, the heads of the two baronial dynasties who dominated the north, the Percys and the Nevilles. The Percys later claimed that Henry swore an oath at Doncaster declaring that he had come only to claim his inheritance, not to molest the King. If this is true it was more probably a stratagem to broaden the base of his support than a statement of real intent.

When the Duke of York, with a small royalist army, gave in to the inevitable and threw in his lot with Henry at Berkeley Castle on 27 July, the outcome was no longer in doubt. Richard, returning from Ireland on the same day, allowed himself to be gulled by assurances that Henry would be content with the restitution of his duchy, and fell into an ambush laid by the Earl of Northumberland's men near Flint. In less than six weeks Henry had made himself master of England. It now remained to take the giant step from de facto master to anointed King.

The manner in which Henry presented his claim was all-important, for any loopholes would quickly be seized upon by Richard and his heirs or by any malcontent baronial clique seeking a respectable pretext for rebellion. Many of Henry's subsequent misfortunes stemmed from precisely the fact that his claim was paper-thin by any measure. He could give out that Richard, now a prisoner in the Tower, had abdicated of his own free will and designated Henry his successor by giving him his signet ring, but how could the story be proved? He could claim by right of conquest, but such a right found no sanction in law. He could claim to have been elected by Lords and Commons, but then he might find his prerogative shackled by conditions imposed in return. He could even fall back on the old wives' tale that his Lancastrian ancestor Edmund was the elder, not the younger, brother of Edward I, and the Crown was being restored to the senior branch of the Plantagenets. In the event, a deliberately vague mixture of all these claims was put before Parliament at the end of September 1399.

Opposite: Henry Bolingbroke, Earl of Derby, Duke of Hereford and Lancaster, the first Lancastrian King of England. Due to the nature of his accession and his tenuous claims to the throne, internal plots and rebellion endangered the early years of Henry IV's reign.

¶ Anno d. mill⁰ ccc⁰ iiii xx xix fuit coron⁅
... wastlond q̄n anno ip̄m ...
... fuit stella comata ...
Slondo̅ m̄spere. iste Henric rex...
A pe̅tit de lyncoln co oleo aq̄...
... eiat p̄ qua ad oleo illo vngeb̅ ...
... se Henr̅ fecit arc̅hm̅ ...
londo̅ patent combu̅ fecit.

fen̅rias princeps   Thos dux clarenc   aut Bedfordie   Wmtrioue dux Gloucestre

Iohanna

fter him regnis thanne.
The iiij henri a doughti man.
At Westeminstur crouned he was.
Wher of all Englond made solas.
... a blysing stere.

Elkan glendore was ante truly.
A doughti man he was and wyse.
In euen bataill he hadde ye prise.
At ye bataill of Shrowisbury tirkl...
Off his enemis he had ye victori.
He regnid here iust most xiiij yere...

Du couronnement du roy henry ·   estoient · Et la fut tout ledit poeu

The coronation of Henry IV, after the imprisoned Richard II's abdication, from the Froissart chronicles. According to one report the service was marred by three bad omens for the future.

Henry's coronation on Monday, 13 October – the feast of the translation of Edward the Confessor – was celebrated in the traditional form, with his eldest son, Henry of Monmouth, bearing the sword of mercy which the new King had himself borne at Richard's crowning. If we are to believe Adam of Usk, a Welsh councillor who wrote a history of Henry's reign, the ceremony was attended by three ill omens for the future: 'First, in the procession, he lost one of his coronation shoes: whence, in the first place, the Commons who rose up against him hated him ever after his whole life long. Secondly, one of the golden spurs fell off: whence, in the second place, the soldiery opposed him in rebellion. Thirdly, at the banquet a sudden gust of wind carried away the crown from his head: whence, in the last place, he was set aside from his kingdom and supplanted by Prince Henry.'

It was the soldiery, or rather the barons whose badges they wore, who struck first. Barely three months of the new reign had elapsed before Henry had to flee from Windsor to London to escape from a rebel coup plotted by the Earls of Kent, Huntingdon and Salisbury and Lord Despenser. All were closely associated with the deposed King and three had recently been deprived of the titles conferred on them by Richard in 1397. But their cause was not yet a popular one and they were beheaded by the mob before they fell into Henry's hands. Some thirty other rebels were executed after the King had presided over their trial at Oxford. Their corpses were chopped up and carted to London in sacks. The ferocity of Henry's response bears witness to the near-panic caused by the revolt of the Earls, a revolt which came so soon after an almost bloodless usurpation. It proved that it was easier to win the throne than to keep it. It also sealed Richard's fate. Although we do not know exactly how or when he died, it must have been with Henry's connivance, if not at his orders. In February 1400 the Council recommended that the body should be publicly exposed in London to scotch any rumours of escape.

The autumn of 1400 saw the start of an intractable guerrilla war in Wales. It began just as a local quarrel between a Welsh squire, Owen Glendower, and his English neighbour, but quickly flared into a national uprising. Glendower's successful resistance was certainly one of the causes of a far more serious crisis which erupted in 1403 with the revolt of Henry's hitherto most powerful supporters, the Percys. The Earl of Northumberland's son, Henry Percy, better known as Hotspur, had taken umbrage when the King refused him the ransom of an important Scottish prisoner, the Earl of Douglas. He also had some grievances about the lack of support he had received while serving as Henry's lieutenant in North Wales. These seem slender grounds for revolt, but Hotspur was a vain, impetuous man and he carried the rest of his family with him. To make matters worse, the Percys were connected with Glendower by marriage – Glendower's daughter was married to Edmund Mortimer, uncle of Richard II's heir and brother of Hotspur's wife.

It was the most testing crisis of Henry's reign and he solved it with his usual speed and decision. He at once marched west to Shrewsbury, which was held by Prince Henry, and there brought Hotspur and his uncle, the Earl of Worcester, to battle before they could join the Earl of Northumberland. The savage battle fought near Shrewsbury on 21 July 1403 ended in a royal victory when Hotspur himself was slain. Worcester was executed two days later but Northumberland was spared after promising to surrender his castles and his office as Constable. Henry's restraint earned him little credit, for the Earl proved an implacable conspirator. Early in 1405 Thomas Mowbray, the Earl Marshal and son of the late Duke of Norfolk, was involved in a plot to spirit the Earl of March away from Windsor to Wales. The fugitives were caught by Henry himself at Cheltenham. The nineteen-year-old Earl of March was pardoned and promptly made off to join Northumberland in another armed rising. In the meantime Northumberland was said to have signed a compact with Glendower and Mortimer partitioning England between them. Richard Scrope, Archbishop of York, was also persuaded to join the plot, and posted on the church doors a manifesto accusing Henry of usurping the throne against his oath, murdering King Richard and levying taxes he had promised to abolish. The rebel army was dispersed and the Archbishop and the Earl Marshal captured by the Neville Earl of Westmorland before Henry arrived. This time there was to be no mercy. A great scandal ensued when not only Mowbray but also the Archbishop were executed, and the unidentified illness which partially paralysed Henry shortly afterwards was said to be God's punishment for this impiety. Northumberland fled to Scotland and was not finally called to account until February 1408, when he died in a skirmish with the Sheriff of Yorkshire's men on Bramham Moor.

After Northumberland's death Henry's throne was secure. The Scottish border had been relatively quiet since 1406, when the young King James I was captured on his way to France. Even the Welsh revolt gradually petered out when Harlech Castle was starved into submission in 1409. The French who had sent troops to Glendower's aid in 1405 were preoccupied with civil war between the rival factions of Burgundy and Armagnac. But the King's health had been broken. From 1406 onwards he was frequently immobilised or bed-ridden by a mysterious disease which contemporaries called leprosy, and in the winter of 1408–9 there were fears for his life. A famous physician was summoned from Lucca, and Henry made his will. No doubt the campaigns of 1399 to 1405 had taken their toll. So too had the burdens which these campaigns imposed on his administrations. To wage war in Scotland and

Wales was prodigiously expensive, and lack of money proved a constant headache. No less than ten treasurers in thirteen years struggled to balance the books, but none succeeded. 'There is not enough money in your treasury to pay the messengers', wrote one of them in 1401. Almost annually between 1400 and 1407 Henry had to endure a running battle with his Commons over the granting of taxes and customs dues. Making capital of Henry's political weak- ness, the Commons aired all their grievances about the extravagance of his household, the membership of his Council, the grants made to his fol- lowers and the uses to which previous subsidies had been put, before assenting to taxation. The Commons did not hate Henry, as Adam of Usk implied, but they certainly treated him to more outspoken criticism than any other medieval king had to face. If Henry resented this, he seldom showed it. He met their demands with patient moderation, always careful to avoid a confrontation.

Gold noble struck during the reign of Henry IV. Campaigns in Wales and Scotland proved extremely expensive and Henry continually struggled with Parliament to gain the additional finance.

Adam of Usk's third point – that Henry was set aside and supplanted by his son – is an exaggeration, but it has a kernel of truth. Until 1407 the Prince had his hands full campaigning in Wales, and enjoyed his father's complete confidence. In the later years of the reign there were signs of tension, and sometimes even of opposition. As the King's health failed his eldest son expected to play a greater role in government. At first, however, Henry IV preferred to entrust his affairs to the veteran Archbishop Arundel, whom he appointed Chancellor. During this time the Prince emerged as the nucleus of an opposition within the Council.

In December 1409 the Chancellor was pressured into resignation and Prince Henry took over as the Council's president. For two years the Prince remained in control, but in November 1411 a serious quarrel with the King brought about the dismissal of his Council and Arundel's return. The causes of the quarrel are obscure, but it seems likely that Henry was goaded into action by the suggestion that he should abdi-

Effigy of Henry IV on his tomb at Canterbury Cathedral. His reign founded a new dynasty and his kingdom passed to his son Henry, Prince of Wales.

cate in the Prince's favour. Polite formality was observed on both sides, but unhappily the matter was not allowed to rest there. In the following May there were rumours that the Prince was raising an army to depose his father, and he felt compelled to write a long letter from Coventry denying the charge. He then came before the King in London with a large following to demand the punishment of his slanderers.

Any further development of this sordid family quarrel was cut short before the year was out by the fact that Henry was obviously dying. By now his face as well as his body was badly disfigured. The end came on 20 March 1413 at Westminster Palace. The Prince was at his side and received his blessing.

So died the first of the Lancastrian kings; an old man at forty-seven, wasted by disease and worn out by the cares of state. The Crown so easily won in 1399 had brought him little joy since. For a king who strove so hard to do the right thing and a man whose strict piety in Church matters is well attested, his misfortune must have seemed a divine punishment for the sin of usurping Richard's throne. 'I Henry, sinful wretch,' he wrote in his will of 1408, '... ask my lords and true people forgiveness if I have misentreated them in any wise.' But his reign cannot be judged a failure. The fact remains that he founded a new dynasty and passed his kingdom intact to his heir. For a usurper this was a considerable feat, particularly in an age when legitimism lay at the heart of political theory and action. The rebel barons had been defeated, Scotland and France neutralised, and the Welsh restored to their allegiance. Even the Commons, for all their reluctance to pay taxes, never questioned Henry's title. Though he was seldom the master of events, he ruled with a mixture of decision, perseverance and tact which few kings could have matched in his place. This achievement goes a long way towards meeting the claim of at least one chronicler, Thomas Walsingham, that Henry IV 'for thirteen and a half years less five days reigned gloriously'.

HENRY V *r. 1413-22*

ENRY IV SUCCEEDED, AGAINST THE ODDS, in founding a royal dynasty; his son, against incalculably greater odds, conquered an empire. Two years from his father's death Henry V destroyed the chivalry of France at Agincourt. Within eight years he entered Paris as Regent of France. Within nine he was dead.

Henry V is a rare example of the men who shape history to their own design. The spectacular achievements of his reign are in a very real sense the achievements of one man. Well before he came to the throne in March 1413 his ability was proven beyond doubt. Created Prince of Wales at his father's coronation in 1399, shortly after his twelfth birthday, he was soon taking an active part in the administration of the principality. When Owen Glendower's rebellion signalled the beginning of a national Welsh uprising in 1400, the Prince's household was established at Chester with Henry Percy as his guardian. Hotspur, a seasoned campaigner in his late thirties, provided Henry's early lessons in the art of war. These stood him in good stead three years later, in 1403, when the fifteen-year-old Prince fought his first pitched battle, with Hotspur, now turned rebel, commanding the opposing army. The battle of Shrewsbury was a viciously contested action, lasting several hours. Henry commanded his father's right and showed his mettle by fighting the day out despite being wounded in the face by an arrow.

The royal victory at Shrewsbury ended Hotspur's career, but Glendower's revolt absorbed the Prince's energies for the next five years. Here he learned the value of a small mobile striking-force to harry his enemy and at the siege of Aberystwyth in 1407 he first experienced the tedium of starving an impregnable fortress into surrender. Constantly

Opposite: Thomas Hoccleve presenting his book, *Regement of Princes*, to the Prince of Wales, later Henry V.

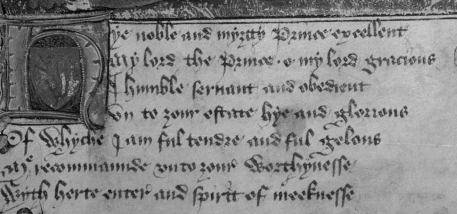

he noble and myȝtty Prince excellent
My lord the Prince o my lord gracious
ȝe humble seruant and obedient
on to ȝoure estate hye and glorious
Of whiche I am ful tendre and ful ȝelous
my recommaunde vnto ȝoure worthynesse
With herte entere and spirit of meeknesse

An early fifteenth-century depiction of Archbishop Arundel. When Henry IV's health began to fail he appointed Arundel to manage the affairs of state, causing a rift between Arundel and Henry, Prince of Wales, who was impatient to take charge.

short of funds with which to pay his troops, he also learned the important of putting war on a proper financial footing.

The Prince did not spend all his time at war in the valleys. From 1406 onwards he was also making his presence felt at meetings of the Council, the body of advisers whom the King selected to run his administration. It was in this year that rumours first began to circulate about the Prince wanting his father to abdicate because of his ill-health. In the winter of 1408–9 Henry very nearly got his way when a particularly bad attack of illness almost killed Henry IV. The Prince had to wait and chafe until the spring of 1410 when he took over as the acknowledged leader of the Council in place of Archbishop Arundel. His father seems to have accepted this situation with some reluctance, and when there was more talk of abdication in the autumn of 1411 he reacted smartly by sacking his son and bringing the Archbishop back as Chancellor. However, the Prince had made a very good impression during his year and a half of office, and afterwards the Commons thanked him handsomely for his efforts.

The differences between the Prince's supporters and Archbishop Arundel's party owed more to temperament and personal loyalties than to political issues. The Archbishop and the Neville Earl of Westmorland represented the older generation, long-time associates of Henry IV, who probably found the Prince's impatience to rule as galling as did the ailing King. They were backed by most of the senior clerics who formed the backbone of any medieval administration. Among the Prince's councillors were two young Earls who shared his taste for military adventure – the Archbishop's own nephew Richard, Earl of Arundel, and Thomas Beauchamp, Earl of Warwick. But Prince Henry's chief support came from his Beaufort half-uncles, Henry and Thomas – John of Gaunt's sons by his third wife, Catherine Swynford. Thomas Beaufort acted as Chancellor while the Prince headed the Council, but his younger brother, Henry, Bishop of Winchester, was the abler of the two, a financial and administrative genius destined to play a leading role in the next two reigns. The Beauforts were shrewd enough to recognise that the future lay with the Prince and backed him accordingly. It was Bishop Henry who took it upon himself to suggest Henry IV's abdication.

There was, however, one political issue with broad implications for the future, on which Prince Henry took an opposite line to Arundel and his father. It concerned France. From the beginning of Henry IV's reign relations with France had been hostile. Charles IV of France, whose daughter had married Richard II, refused to recognise Henry IV as King, and when Henry sent the widowed Isabella back to France in 1400 he declined to part with her jewellery. The French renewed their claims to the Duchy of Aquitaine, raided Calais and sent help to Glendower in Wales. But these attacks were ill co-ordinated and half-hearted. Charles VI suffered from frequent bouts of insanity during which his brother, the Duke of Orleans, and his cousin, the Duke of Burgundy, fell to quarrelling. In 1407 the quarrel degenerated into civil war when the Duke of Orleans was assassinated at the instigation of his Burgundian rival, John the Fearless. For the English, hitherto paralysed by their own internal problems, this was a heaven-sent opportunity to divide and conquer. The only problem was which side England should choose as her ally against the other. Henry IV favoured the Orleans faction who called themselves the Armagnacs; his son preferred the Burgundian alliance.

In October 1411, while the Prince still controlled the Council, an English expedition commanded by the Earl of Arundel sailed to Burgundy's aid. But when the Prince was dismissed English policy went into reverse, and in 1412 his brother, Prince Thomas, crossed to Normandy at the head of a much larger army to help the Armagnacs. This second expedition was intimately bound up with the ill feeling between the Prince of Wales and the King. Prince Thomas, now created

Thomas Beauchamp, Earl of Warwick is knighted by King Henry IV. Warwick was an ardent supporter of Henry Prince of Wales and shared his taste for military adventure.

Henry V pays homage to King Charles VI of France. Henry confirmed his military success in the Treaty of Troyes signed with Charles in 1420. This agreement made Henry Regent of France and heir to the throne of Valois.

Duke of Clarence, had sided with his father and was thus chosen to command in his elder brother's place. Prince Henry refused to go and was accused of staying behind in order to stage a coup. His opponents at court also charged him with misappropriating funds intended for the defence of Calais. The Prince responded by sending a stream of messengers to important people explaining his case, and won from his father a promise to have the accusations against him examined in Parliament. In September 1412 he appeared in London with such 'a huge people' of retainers that fears of an armed take-over were again aroused.

Whatever we make of the poorly documented events of Henry IV's last year, it does seem that the King's final illness and death defused a potentially dangerous situation, with the royal family and the aristocracy splitting into factions, mutual accusations of disloyalty and malpractice,

Contemporary depiction of the battle of Agincourt, 25 October 1415, from a manuscript by the chronicler Jean Froissart. For the next five years Henry concentrated all his energies on completing his French conquests.

and retainers gathering to protect their lords. It also appears that Prince Henry behaved with an arrogance born out of the absolute conviction that he was in the right.

When the old King was finally dead and the Prince crowned Henry V, the atmosphere changed markedly for the better. Among the new King's first concerns was to extend the olive branch to those who had suffered under the previous reign. The Earl of March, whose father had been named as Richard II's heir, had his estates restored to him, the Earls of Huntingdon and Oxford were returned to favour, and the body of Richard II was reburied with pomp at Westminster. Perhaps Henry retained some affection for the murdered King who had taken him to

Ireland in 1399 but declined to use the boy as a hostage when his father came to seize Richard's throne. But it was also a shrewd piece of propaganda, a call to bury old grievances and rally round to Henry's grand design – the conquest of France. The policy paid off, for two years later the only aristocratic conspiracy of Henry's reign was reported to the King by the Earl of March himself.

Clarence's expedition of 1412 had achieved nothing: as soon as he landed the Armagnacs changed their minds about seeking English help and bought him off. Henry still preferred the Burgundian alliance, but this time he was less eager to show his hand. He negotiated with the Armagnacs as well, forcing them to outbid their rivals for England's support or neutrality. Early in 1415 the Armagnacs offered him substantial territorial concessions in Aquitaine and the hand of Charles VI's daughter, Catherine, along with a dowry of 600,000 crowns. But Henry wanted much more than that. He told them he would settle for nothing less than the whole of the old Angevin Empire, lost in the reign of King John, including Normandy, Maine and Anjou. The extravagance of this claim, which no French government could possibly accept, suggests that the negotiations were just diplomatic window dressing. Henry had already made up his mind to go to war. By the time negotiations were broken off in June 1415 Parliament had already voted a double subsidy for the campaign, an army had been raised and the necessary transport requisitioned.

On 11 August Henry sailed from Southampton with an army of about 10,000 archers and men-at-arms. The army landed on the Norman coast and spent the first month of the campaign besieging Harfleur, which surrendered on 22 September. By now the season was too far gone for a march on Paris, and Henry settled for a cross-country march to Calais. Shortly after crossing the Somme he found his way blocked at Agincourt by a French army which outnumbered his own by three to one. On 25 October the two armies faced one another in a pitched battle, the French cavalry attacking the English archers in a massed charge on a narrow front. These disastrous tactics ended in a bloodbath for the chivalry of France, who lost perhaps 6,000 men dead and many more captured. Henry lost fewer than four hundred, including the Duke of York and the Earl of Suffolk.

The march to Calais had been a grave strategic risk, again the action of a man who never experienced an iota of self-doubt. The rewards were stupendous, not only in France where his bargaining position was

Following pages: The battle of Agincourt, at which Henry V destroyed the chivalry of France in a pitched battle that left some 6,000 French dead at a cost of 400 English lives.

33

Letter in the hand of Henry v discussing French prisoners captured at Agincourt. Controversially, at one point during the battle the heavily outnumbered Henry ordered the execution of some French prisoners. The order was soon countermanded when it became obvious that there would be no further French attacks.

Opposite: The Emperor Sigismund, Holy Roman Emperor, King of Hungary and Bohemia. In 1416 Sigismund signed the Treaty of Canterbury with Henry v, thereby supporting Henry's claim to the French throne.

immensely strengthened, but at home too where his people were now united to a man behind their victorious King. Agincourt achieved in a single day the goal which Henry IV had laboured for thirteen years to attain. For the next five years England's energies were harnessed exclusively to the completion of Henry's French conquests.

The task which confronted the King was still formidable. Pitched battles were rare in medieval warfare and after Agincourt the French were far too respectful of Henry's prowess to risk a second annihilation. The conquest of Normandy was to be a lengthy and tedious catalogue of sieges, of towns battered, starved or terrified into submission. This was a radical departure from the traditional forms of the Hundred Years' War – the large-scale mounted raids or *chevauchees* which devastated the countryside in search of plunder. From the very beginning Henry came in the guise of France's rightful King, determined to establish a permanent English presence in the country he subdued.

Before the second expedition sailed in 1417 the King achieved a notable diplomatic triumph. For four months in 1416 Henry entertained the Holy Roman Emperor, Sigismund, who arrived as a mediator and departed as an ally after putting his name to the Treaty of Canterbury. The treaty is proof of how well Henry argued his claim to the French Crown and dispelled the notion that he was a military adventurer taking advantage of the civil war distracting his neighbours. In October 1416 the two monarchs conferred with Duke John of Burgundy at Calais.

On 1 August 1417 Henry set foot in Normandy again. Caen fell in September, followed by Verneuil and Falaise before Christmas. John the Fearless fulfilled his part of the bargain struck at Calais by threatening Paris from the north. By August 1418 the English controlled the whole of Lower Normandy and Henry had invested the key target of Rouen. The Norman capital was too strong for an assault, but the city finally succumbed to starvation in January 1419. The remainder of the resistance throughout Normandy crumbled and by spring Henry was master of the whole Duchy.

At this point diplomacy again took precedence over military affairs. In July 1419 Henry's successes were seriously threatened by a reconciliation between the Burgundians and the Armagnacs (now known as the Dauphinists). But Henry's luck held. The murder of the Duke of Burgundy by the Dauphin's men on 10 September 1419 showed that the mutual hatred of the French factions was still more powerful than their fear of the English aggressor. The Burgundians were now ready to pay any price for Henry's alliance. By Christmas Philip, the new Duke of Burgundy, had given way to all Henry's demands: the mad Charles VI would retain the Crown during his lifetime but Henry would be recognised as his heir and would marry his daughter Catherine. In return Henry was pledged to avenge the previous Duke's murder and make war on the Dauphin, who still controlled most of France south of the Loire. These terms were embodied in the Treaty of Troyes in May 1420. On 2 June the King and Catherine were married at the altar of Troyes Cathedral, and on 1 December the royal couple entered Paris in triumph.

Henry had been absent from England for three and a half years when he returned in February 1421 for the Queen's coronation. A royal progress followed which took the couple through Bristol, the Welsh Marches and Leicester to the northern capital of York, then back to

The siege of Rouen: the town proved too strong for an assault and was starved into submission in 1419, thus completing Henry's conquest of Normandy.

Opposite: The Duke of Burgundy driven from the walls of Calais. Henry supported an alliance with the Burgundians to aid his operations in Normandy.

In 1420 Henry married Catherine, the daughter of Charles VI of France, in Troyes Cathedral. Her dowry was 600,000 crowns.

Opposite: Henry v and courtiers depicted within the initial 'h'. From the *Cartae Antiquae*, a late fifteenth-century collection of statutes.

Westminster by way of Lincoln and Norwich. It was a brief and doubtless welcome respite, during which the Queen conceived the future Henry VI. But whatever pleasure it gave the King was cut short by the news of his brother Clarence's death on a raid in the Loire country – a bitter and timely reminder that his task in France was still only half done.

In June he returned to the wars, and the winter months passed in the protracted siege of Meaux, one of the last Dauphinist strongpoints north of the Loire. The town's capitulation in May 1422 was to be Henry's last triumph. During the winter he contracted an illness – probably dysentery – which he could not shake off. In July he had to be carried in a litter to the siege of Cosne on the Loire. A few days later he had to turn back, and in the early morning of 31 August he died at Bois de Vincennes.

How can one assess the tremendous achievement of Henry v's nine short years as King? Certainly he owed a great deal to luck and circumstance. At Agincourt the blundering tactics of the French contributed as much to the English victory as did Henry's generalship. His subsequent successes could not have been achieved without the internecine hatred of the two French factions. As one contemporary cynic noted, the English entered Paris through the hole in the Duke of Burgundy's skull.

But Henry was much more than a soldier with fortune on his side. He was a statesman with a range of exceptional talents which enabled him to bend fortune to his ends. Like Napoleon, Henry v was a glutton for hard work and no detail concerning the administration of his conquests was beneath his notice. The logistical effort of supplying the army of 1417 on foreign soil for more than three years was a feat in itself equal to the victory of Agincourt. During his campaigns in France he insisted even on dealing personally with all petitions forwarded from

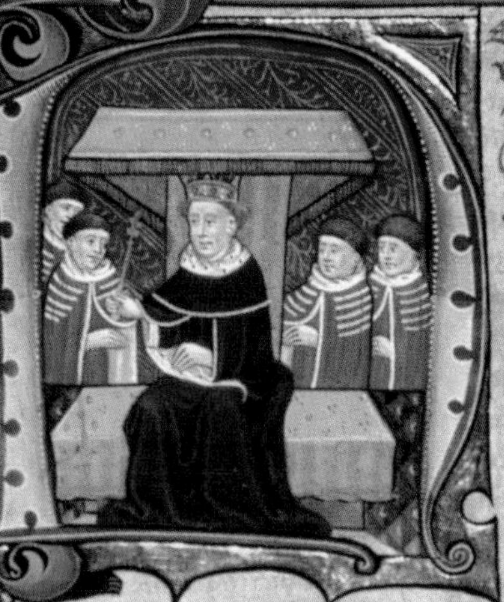

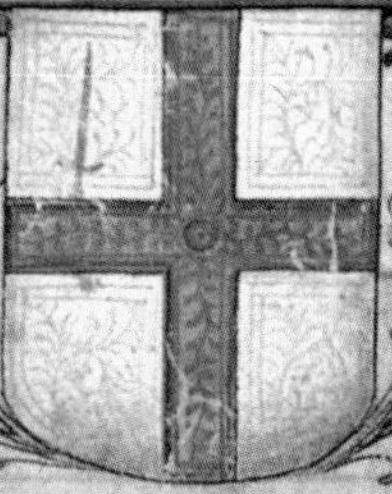

his Parliaments in England. Contemporaries, his enemies as much as his friends, were profoundly struck by Henry's sense of justice, which was linked with a strict adherence to the tenets of Catholic piety. As Prince of Wales he had personally presided over the funeral pyre of an unrepentant Lollard – one of those proto-Protestants who foreshadowed the Reformation of the succeeding century. On the way to Agincourt he had a man hanged for robbing a church. 'He was a Prince of Justice', wrote the Burgundian chronicler Chastellain, 'he gave support to none out of favour, nor did he suffer wrong to go unpunished out of regard for affinity'. Underlying all Henry's qualities was his ironclad will-power which not only drove him but also provided the inspiration for others. He gathered around him a team of outstanding military and administrative ability, most notably his Beaufort uncles and his brothers, Thomas the soldier and John, Duke of Bedford, who became Regent of France on Henry's death. No other fifteenth-century king was so ably or so devotedly served, and indeed most found more reason to fear their relatives than to favour them. Another Frenchman observed shrewdly that Henry did not look like a soldier at all, but rather possessed the gravity of a cleric. This view is confirmed by his portraits which reveal a lean, hatchet face dominated by sombre brown eyes, pursed lips and a long thin nose. The face contains more than a hint of the fanatic, so impatient to supplant his father and subordinate himself to the single obsession of conquering France. He certainly had little time to spare during his reign for any private life or domestic comforts. Even on his deathbed he was immersed in plans and provisions for his son's minority, without seeking or receiving a visit from the child's mother. There is a frightening quality about this all-conquering, all-competent zealot, which could account for the legends which sprang up after his death of his wild and boisterous youth as Prince of Wales. These tales lend to his character a posthumous humanity not apparent in life.

Perhaps Henry was lucky to die young and pass straight into legend. Even before his death there are signs that his heroic designs were parting company with his country's interests. The Commons were complaining of his long absences. From 1420 grants from Parliament to prosecute the wars were proving hard to come by. The Dauphin was still master of more than half of France and future success depended on the continuing split between his party and the Burgundians. It was a heavy inheritance to leave in the care of the nine-month-old infant, Henry VI.

Opposite: Effigy of Henry V in Westminster Abbey. An inspirational and spiritual King, at the time of his death in August 1422, Henry had triumphed over France and passed into legend.

HENRY VI *r.* 1422–71

OME FIFTY YEARS AFTER HENRY V was laid to rest, a lonely old man was quietly done to death in the Tower of London after he had lost his wits, his two kingdoms and his only son. Everything about the reign of Henry VI is in stark contrast to that of his father. But the first and most striking contrast is that whereas the father had to wait with ill-concealed impatience for his inheritance, the son had his thrust upon him before he was one year old.

From the earliest age Henry was frequently paraded at public ceremonies, either seated on his mother's lap or tottering on his own feet between his royal relatives. As he grew up he saw progressively less of the Queen, who had formed a liaison with a Welsh squire named Owen Tudor and was busy raising a second family. In 1428 he was placed in the care of Richard Beauchamp, Earl of Warwick, and one of his father's most trusted lieutenants. Warwick was instructed to 'teach him nurture, literature, language and the manner of cunning, to chastise him when he doth amiss and to remove persons not behoveful nor expedient from his presence'. Henry proved himself a precocious child. At the age of ten, so his governor reported, he was questioning whether he, a king, should be chastised for his misdemeanours and taking an interest in matters 'not behoveful'. The Council was called in to read the riot act.

At a tender age the boy King was introduced to the most intractable problems of his early reign – the deteriorating situation in France and the unedifying squabbles of those closest to the throne. The emergence of Joan of Arc and the crowning of the Dauphin as Charles VII at Rheims in 1429 heralded the Valois revival. Bedford, the English Regent in France, was sufficiently worried to call for his nephew's coronation

Opposite: A portrait, *c.* 1550, of Henry VI, who succeeded to the throne before he was a year old, and whose reign was to prove so tragically different from that of his illustrious father.

and to bring him over to France for a state visit. On 2 December 1431 Henry was crowned King of France at St Denis in Paris. However, the tide had turned against the English. Duke Philip of Burgundy knew it and was looking for a way out of his alliance. In 1435 he made his separate peace with Charles VII at Arras; in the same year the valiant Bedford, whose earlier successes had almost matched those of Henry V, breathed his last. From that point it was all downhill. When Henry heard of Burgundy's desertion he burst into tears.

At home the trouble was caused by Henry's other and infinitely less able uncle, Humphrey, Duke of Gloucester. Gloucester was a fine scholar but a poor statesman. Though he was nominated Regent of England in Henry v's will, his peers distrusted him sufficiently to insist that he govern with the advice of the Council, not as Regent but as Protector. He quarrelled incessantly with that other pillar of the Lancastrian establishment, the portly Bishop Beaufort, and twice, in 1425 and 1432, their animosity threatened an outbreak of violence. In 1434 Gloucester even picked a quarrel with his brother Bedford, accusing him of mismanaging the war. Henry, in an early display of well-meant but flat-footed conciliation, attempted to mediate between his uncles in person and declared both parties innocent of blame.

Despite their differences the Council did see Henry safely through his minority, which came to an end without a formal declaration to that

Henry VI being crowned King of England in Westminster Abbey. His coronation as King of France took place at St Denis in Paris, making him the only sovereign to have been crowned both in England and France.

Following pages: German tapestry depicting Joan of Arc arriving at the Chateau of Chinon in 1428 during her campaign to end English control of French territory.

effect in 1437. The story of the next thirteen years is such a dreary record of infighting at court, disorder in the shires and reverses in France that one is tempted to dwell instead on the anecdotes of Henry's Christian virtues compiled by his biographer and one-time confessor, John Blacman. It is true that he displayed qualities which would have done credit to a monk or a mendicant friar, and that his two great foundations, at Eton and King's College, Cambridge, in 1440 and 1441, still preserve his memory. He was chaste, pious and generous. He abhorred all forms of bloodshed, and intervened frequently to spare the lives of criminals and traitors. On one occasion, while riding through Cripplegate into London, 'he saw over the gate there the quarter of a man on a tall stake, and asked what it was. And when his lords made answer that it was the quarter of a traitor of his … he said, "Take it away. I will not have any Christian man so cruelly handled for my sake"'. This story, and others like it, have been much quoted by Henry's admirers, who see him as a man dragged down by the coarse spirit of his time.

But the truth is that even Blacman's eulogies sometimes cast Henry in a faintly ridiculous, if not downright foolish, light. He stormed out in a huff one Christmas when 'a certain great lord brought before him a dance or show of young ladies with bared bosoms'. He rebuked the scholars of Eton for visiting his own court over the Thames at Windsor 'bidding them not to do so again, lest his young lambs should come to relish the corrupt deeds and habits of his courtiers'. As a youth he spied on his servants 'through hidden windows of his chamber, lest any foolish impertinence of women coming into the house should … cause the fall of any of his household'. 'From his youth up he always wore round-toed shoes and boots like a farmer's … a long gown with a rolled hood like a townsman, and a full coat reaching below his knees,

An open-air lecture at New College, Oxford, in 1463. Henry's founding of Eton and King's College, Cambridge, point to the increasing importance of education in the age.

Opposite: John, Duke of Bedford, praying before St George. Bedford was Regent of France from the death of Henry V until the coronation of Henry VI.

with shoes, boots and footgear wholly black, rejecting expressly all fashion of clothing.' On feast days, when custom demanded that he wear the crown, Henry atoned with a hair shirt next to his skin.

So it goes on. These were not the attributes of a king and the truth is that Henry had no real wish to act like one. His impatience with secular affairs emerges from another Blacman story: when 'a certain mighty duke' knocked at his door the King complained to his confessor, 'they do so interrupt me that by day or night I can hardly snatch a moment to be refreshed without disturbance'. There lay one half of the coming tragedy. The King was the linchpin of medieval government. It was not just a quaint custom that even during Henry's infancy official documents referred to him as King in fact as well as name. His job was to initiate, to unite, to inspire – the very things that made Henry V such a success. Henry VI proved himself incapable of all three.

There was, however, one regal function which Henry could not lay aside. A vast range of patronage – from the great offices of state to the smallest perks of feudal law – lay at his disposal and had to be disposed. This was the other half of the tragedy. Henry gave too freely and he often gave to the wrong people. The result was that after 1437 the executive power of the Crown fell into the hands of a narrow clique of men who had access to Henry. Two of these were William de la Pole, fourth Earl of Suffolk, and William Ayscough, Bishop of Salisbury. Both rose to eminence because of the key positions they occupied in the King's household. Suffolk, a veteran soldier with fourteen years' continuous service in France to his credit, became Henry's Steward in 1435 and the Bishop was his confessor. Henry's great-uncle, Bishop Beaufort, also retained his influence until his retirement from political life in 1443 at the ripe old age of sixty-seven. These men were soon under attack for their excessive influence over the King, and resorted to some fairly shady manoeuvring in order to retain their monopoly. In 1439 Gloucester complained to the King that Beaufort and his friends had cut off 'me, your sole uncle, together with my cousin of York ... and many other lords of your kin from having knowledge of any great matters that might touch your high estate and realm'. In the summer of 1441 the King's advisers replied with an accusation of sorcery against Gloucester's wife, Eleanor. The Duchess was forced to undergo public penance in the streets of London, and Gloucester, though not directly involved, was neatly discredited.

Opposite: Contemporary French portrait of Charles VII, King of France. In 1450 he regained possession of the Duchy of Normandy, signalling the beginning of the end for English rule in France.

Henry VI investing John Talbot, Earl of Shrewsbury, who is pictured taking the sword of office, as constable of France in 1436.

France was still the burning political issue of the day, with Henry's advisers favouring a peaceful accommodation while Gloucester followed a hawkish line which endeared him to the London mob. The doves of course prevailed and in 1444 Suffolk secured his ascendancy at court by arranging for Henry to marry Charles VII's niece, the fifteen-year-old Margaret of Anjou. The King gratefully added a marquisate to the long list of Suffolk's preferments. Unhappily the result of the marriage was not a lasting peace with France but the renewal of war which led speedily to the loss of all English territories in France save Calais. Margaret was carefully briefed before arrival to work on her future husband and persuade him to surrender the county of Maine. Henry duly promised to do so, but without telling anybody. When the news leaked out, it was greeted with a surge of patriotic outrage. The spring Parliament of 1447 had to meet in Bury rather than risk the fury of the Londoners, and Gloucester was arrested on arrival to be charged with planning an uprising. His death in confinement a week later quickly gave rise to rumours that Suffolk had ordered his murder. To retrieve his tarnished reputation at home, Suffolk suddenly turned hawk in France and launched a provocative attack on Charles VII's ally, the Duke of Brittany. Charles at once retaliated by invading Normandy. Rouen fell in October 1449, Caen in the following July, and by September the whole Duchy was in French hands. In 1451 Charles turned on Gascony and took Bordeaux. Two years later a relieving force under the Earl of Talbot was cut to pieces at Castillon. The Duchy of Aquitaine, after nearly 300 years in England's possession, was lost for ever.

Not even Henry could save Suffolk from the repercussions of the loss of Normandy. In February 1450 the King's 'priviest and best trusted' adviser was impeached in Parliament, charged with every sort of mis-

Henry VI with his Margaret of Anjou, the niece of Charles VII. The kneeling figure presenting a book to the Queen is John Talbot, Earl of Shrewsbury, who would himself suffer when the marriage failed to bring lasting peace.

michi peccatori et prebuit mihi vbi
placet + siuit in oculis maiestatis
tue videtur de me peccatore ita fiat.

AR Rex henricus pauper + ecclesie defensor
ad iram semper pauus incantate feruidus
pietati deditus clerum decorauit, quem dicit
sic beatificauit. VD: A p nobis deuote
henrice RCt digni efficiamur promissio
nibus xpi. Oremus. ORAND

management and embezzlement. Henry did his best to get him out of harm's way by banishing his favourite, but the ship carrying him to safety was intercepted in the Channel and Suffolk was executed on the spot. In truth he deserved little better, and not only because his bungling brought about the catastrophe in France. For years he had been feathering his nest while Henry's Exchequer plunged into debt. He had presided over a general slackening of control at the centre which in turn bred lawlessness, corruption and unrest throughout the kingdom. His most fitting memorial is the Kentish rising known as Cade's Rebellion, which exploded shortly after his death in May 1450. The rebels' chief demand was for the punishment of 'the false progeny and affinity of the Duke of Suffolk'. 'His false council', they concluded, 'has lost his (the King's) law: his merchandise is lost: his common people are destroyed: France is lost. The King himself is so placed that he may not pay for his drink.' 'In this same time', wrote a later chronicler, 'the realm of England was out of all good governance, as it had been many days before, for the King was simple, and led by covetous counsel, and owed more than he was worth.'

It would be foolish to follow the polite fiction of the time and exonerate Henry of all blame for these events. Government was in the hands of the men he himself had chosen. There was no lack of critics to tell him what was wrong. Nor was he incapable of action: he would intervene readily enough when his favourites came under fire. The best that can be said of Henry is that he was quite exceptionally naive.

The disaster which overtook Suffolk did nothing to open the King's eyes. In August his defeated lieutenant in France, Edmund Beaufort, Duke of Somerset, returned to London and stepped into the vacant niche of court favourite. Somerset was a nephew of the departed Bishop and associate of Suffolk. It was bad enough that the new favourite should be tainted by failure in France and friendship with Suffolk's circle: but more serious in the long term was Somerset's long-standing personal feud with Richard, Duke of York, the greatest landowner in England after the King, who had long been at the losing end of a running fight with the Beauforts over the conduct of the war. As a supporter of the Duke of Gloucester he had been excluded from Henry's charmed circle, and in 1449 his opponents had him appointed Lieutenant of Ireland for ten years in order to get him out of the way. In 1450 he returned from his post without permission to take up the cudgels with his rival Duke.

Opposite: King Henry VI depicted in a 15th-century book of hours; and certainly some of his most pressing concerns seem to have been other-worldly.

Their rivalry was all the keener for the fact that both Dukes stood a good chance of inheriting the throne. Margaret had as yet borne no children. Somerset was descended from John of Gaunt and although the Beauforts had been barred from the succession by Parliament in Henry IV's reign, the Act was not immutable. York was descended from Gaunt's elder brother, Lionel, through his mother, Anne Mortimer, and from Gaunt's younger brother, Edmund, through his father, Richard, Earl of Cambridge. From the confrontation of these two men sprang the Wars of the Roses.

For the next three years (1450–53) the court party, headed by Somerset, successfully resisted all York's attempts to dislodge them. When the Member for Bristol suggested in the Commons that York should be recognised as Henry's heir, he was promptly sent to the Tower. In the spring of 1452 York actually marched on London with an army at his back. Somerset quickly assembled a larger force and barred the way at Dartford. On this occasion bloodshed was avoided by trickery. York agreed to dismiss his force on condition that Somerset should be arrested and called to account for his misdoings in Normandy. But when York allowed himself to be brought into Henry's tent, he found himself a prisoner. Somerset wisely refrained from putting his enemy on trial, for popular sympathy favoured York. The Duke was released after swearing never again to take up arms against any of Henry's subjects.

In 1453 came several dramatic reversals of fortune. First, the Hundred Years' War came to an end with Talbot's annihilation at Castillon, and Henry's government was once more held to blame. In August the King suffered the first of those bouts of insanity that were to recur throughout the rest of his life. His illness reduced him to a state of paralytic melancholia, depriving him of memory, speech and reason. For this he had to thank the genes inherited from his mad grandfather, Charles VI of France. It is ironic that only two months later the House of Lancaster was blessed with the birth of a male heir. After eight barren years of marriage Queen Margaret presented her afflicted husband with a son. Prince Edward was shown to the King for his blessing at Windsor on New Year's Day 1454 'in vain, for they departed thence without any answer or countenance, saving only that once he looked upon the Prince and cast down his eyes again, without any more'.

Henry and Margaret were in many respects a most ill-suited pair. In contrast to his ineffectual, other-worldly nature she was a tigress, quick-tempered, courageous and passionate in both her likes and dis-

likes. She cannot have found Henry a very attentive husband. In the early years of their marriage the rumour was that the King's confessor and councillor, Bishop Ayscough, was responsible for dissuading him from having 'his sport' with the Queen, advising Henry not to 'come nigh her'. Given Henry's prudish views on sex and nudity it is doubtful whether he needed much persuading. When he recovered from his first madness he himself expressed bewilderment at the birth of his son, who, he said, must have been conceived by the Holy Ghost.

Notwithstanding their incompatibility, the Queen was a powerful force in the world of politics. Henry was putty in her hands when she wanted something done, and she developed a fierce, almost partisan, loyalty to his chief ministers: first Suffolk, whom she treated as a father; then Somerset, who was accused of being her lover. Equally fierce was Margaret's dislike of York, whom she saw not as the self-styled victim of Somerset's wiles, but as an arrogant aggressor intent on destroying herself, her husband and her son. She was, as it happened, proved absolutely right, but it was her own implacable hostility towards York that converted him from the one to the other.

Ironically, York first tasted power soon after Prince Edward's birth knocked him out of the succession. With the King unfit to rule there was

A medal by Pietro da Milano depicting Margaret of Anjou, the niece of Charles VII of France, who was married to Henry when she was fifteen.

nothing Margaret or Somerset could do to prevent York's appointment as Protector in March 1454. Somerset was arrested (in the Queen's apartments), impeached and committed to the Tower. Towards Christmas the King recovered, and in February 1455 York was dismissed, Somerset restored. Mutual hatred and suspicion were by now so entrenched that a recourse to arms became inevitable. York's appeals to the King were suppressed by Henry's courtiers. On 22 May 1455 a Yorkist force confronted Somerset and the King at St Albans. Parleying broke down when Henry refused to surrender the Duke of Somerset. Within an hour the battle was lost, Somerset was dead, and the King, his neck grazed by an arrow, meekly allowed the victor to renew his oath of allegiance.

Despite the bloodshed a settlement should now have been possible. It would be wrong to think that the peerage was irrevocably split into two hostile factions, the Yorkists on one side, Lancastrians on the other. The men who backed York – including the powerful Richard Neville, Earl of Warwick – did so not because they wanted to make him King in Henry's place, but because of their various private grudges against members of the court circle. With Somerset out of the way most peers favoured conciliation, and Henry himself certainly had no wish to propagate a blood feud.

Queen Margaret unfortunately took a very different view, and it was she who prevailed. The heirs of the men who had fallen at St Albans readily supported her and soon the two leading northern families, the Nevilles and the Percys, were at each other's throats again. In March 1458 Henry, on his own initiative, made a remarkable effort to forestall another explosion of violence. At a special ceremony of reconciliation all the chief protagonists, including Margaret and York, marched hand in hand to St Paul's behind the King.

This was all a charade. In the summer of 1459 Margaret raised another army and marched on York's stronghold of Ludlow in the Welsh Marches. This time the Yorkists were routed: the Duke fled to Ireland, the Earl of Salisbury, his son Warwick and York's heir Edward, Earl of March, to Calais. The Calais contingent reappeared in the summer of 1460 and in turn routed the royal army at the battle of Northampton. This time York was in no mood for further compromise. It was clear that while Margaret ruled the King any compromise would simply be undone the moment the court party felt strong enough to renege on it. Accordingly, in October, York submitted to Parliament his claim to the throne of England.

Opposite: The Neville family at prayer from the Neville Book of Hours. The Nevilles were one of the most powerful families in the north of England, strong supporters of Richard, Duke of York.

Edward, Earl of March, flees England for Calais in 1459. Edward, who was the Yorkist heir to the throne, is accompanied by his uncle the Earl of Salisbury and his cousin the Earl of Warwick.

It looked as though a repeat performance of 1399 was about to be enacted. However, the Lords, including even the two Neville Earls, were not yet ready to sanction such a revolutionary move. It was agreed instead that Henry should remain King for life, but recognise York as his heir. Henry seems to have acquiesced in the disinheriting of his son. Not so Margaret, who had eluded capture at Northampton and taken refuge with the Prince behind the battlements of Harlech Castle. In a fine display of martial courage she took ship for Berwick on the Scottish border and appeared in mid-December at the head of a new Lancastrian host. York and Salisbury hurried north with a small force to meet the threat and rashly committed themselves to battle without waiting for reinforcements. On 30 December 1460 York's army was crushed at Wakefield. The Duke himself died on the battlefield, and his head was later displayed on the gates of York wearing a paper crown.

In 1461, the final year of Henry's reign, events came thick and fast. As Margaret marched on London, St Albans was the scene of a second battle at which Warwick was defeated and the King restored to his wife. Nevertheless, London's gates remained closed, its citizens fearful of the looting which might ensure if Margaret's northerners gained

The capture of Henry VI by the forces of Richard, Earl of Warwick, after the battle of Northampton in 1460.

admittance. Warwick managed to join his mauled troops with those of York's eldest son, Edward, who entered London in triumph, and was installed as King in Westminster Abbey on 4 March. Henry and Margaret withdrew towards Yorkshire, with Edward at their heels. On 29 March the two armies fought it out near Towton in a blizzard of wind and snow. It was a bloody engagement and ended in the massacre of Margaret's soldiers. The King and Queen took refuge over the border in Scotland.

Nine years were to pass before Henry regained his throne. The story is briefly told, for it is really an epilogue to his reign. For three years he hovered on the outskirts of his lost kingdom at Harlech and at the Northumberland fortress towns of Berwick and Bamburgh, while Margaret schemed to enlist the Scots and the French in his cause. Some minor successes were achieved in the north with the help of Piers de Breze, a renowned French captain on loan from Margaret's cousin Louis XI, but there was not enough money or manpower to pose a serious threat. By the summer of 1463 even Margaret was sufficiently discouraged to return to France with her French allies and her son, leaving Henry precariously ensconced at Bamburgh. Hopes flared again the following spring when the dwindling rump of Lancastrian leaders attempted a rising in Northumberland, but they were trounced at Hexham by Warwick's brother, Lord Montagu. The fall of Bamburgh in the summer deprived Henry of his last stronghold and he seems to have spent the best part of the next year as a wandering fugitive. He was finally picked up near Clitheroe, Lancashire, in July 1465, from where, in Blacman's words, 'he was brought as a traitor and criminal to London, and imprisoned in the Tower there; where, like a true follower of Christ, he patiently endured hunger, thirst, mockings, derisions, abuse and many other hardships'.

And so at last to the bizarre episode of Henry's restoration, the so-called Readeption of Henry VI. The background details belong more properly to the reign of Edward IV. Suffice it to say that on Wednesday, 3 October 1470 the astonished Henry – 'not cleanly kept as should seem such a Prince' – was suddenly transferred to the luxuriously furnished apartments of Edward IV's Queen and addressed once again as King. Three days later his former adversary, the Earl of Warwick, knelt before him to ask forgiveness. Later Henry, dressed in a long blue gown, was conveyed to St Paul's to give thanks for his delivery. At his new quarters in the Bishop of London's palace in Fulham Henry learned from

Opposite: An illustration from a law treatise of Henry VI's reign, showing the Court of the King's Bench at Westminster. At the top sit five presiding judges, and below them the King's attorney, the coroner and masters of the court. A prisoner stands at the bar, six more in the foreground.

Warwick the details of the Earl's quarrel with Edward IV, of Edward's flight to Burgundy and of the Kingmaker's reconciliation with Queen Margaret at Angers Cathedral. In the following month Warwick's episcopal brother George opened Parliament with an address on the text, taken from the Book of Jeremiah, 'Return, O back-sliding children'. In December came news from France that Prince Edward had married Anne Neville, Warwick's fifteen-year-old daughter.

Throughout the Readeption Henry remained, as always, a puppet, while Warwick pulled the strings. In the words of one chronicler, 'the King was as mute as a crowned calf'. His one act was to send food and clothing to Edward IV's abandoned wife who was about to give birth in the Sanctuary of Westminster Abbey. He never saw his own family again. In March Edward IV landed in Yorkshire, and on 11 April, having outmanoeuvred Warwick, he re-entered London. Two days later Henry was compelled to join Edward's army on the road to Barnet, where on Easter Sunday, Warwick's army was put to flight and the Kingmaker slain. On the same day Queen Margaret landed too late in Weymouth, to be defeated in her turn some three weeks later at Tewkesbury. The seventeen-year-old Prince Edward was among the dead. Margaret was brought back to London and lodged in the Tower, though not in Henry's company.

Henry's captivity ended on the night of 21 May, the day Edward returned to the capital from his victory at Tewkesbury. The chronicler Henry Warkworth recorded that he 'was put to death ... between eleven and twelve of the clock, being then at the Tower ... the Duke of Gloucester ... and many other; and on the morrow he was chested and brought to St Paul's, and his face was open that every man might see him ...' Later he was buried in the Lady Chapel at Chertsey Abbey.

Henry was killed because the magic of his name could still inspire the respect and loyalty which men like Warwick needed as a cloak for their ambitions. His execution was an act of state designed to prevent further rebellion in his name. Even in those blood-soaked days it aroused a shiver of horror among contemporaries, who pointed to Henry's blameless conduct, his charity and his devotion to God. His burial-place soon became a shrine, and it was later said that Richard III moved the body to St George's, Windsor, to put a stop to the pilgrimages and the talk of miracles. Yet Henry must take his share of responsibility for the events which brought him down. The Wars of the Roses sprang from his failure to meet the enormous demands of

Opposite: The Court of the Exchequer as depicted in the Whaddon folio *c.* 1460.

66

medieval kingship. If the man was a saint, the King was a political sim-
pleton, who would neither provide leadership nor delegate it to those
who could.

A fitting epitaph is the poem Henry wrote himself:

> Kingdoms are but cares,
> > State is devoid of stay,
> Riches are ready snares,
> > And hasten to decay.
>
> Pleasure is a privy prick
> > Which vice doth still provoke;
> Pomp, imprompt; and fame, a flame;
> > Power, a smouldering smoke.
>
> Who meanth to remove the rock
> > Owt of the slimy mud,
> Shall mire himself, and hardly scape
> > The swelling of the flood.

Opposite: The Court of
Chancery as depicted in the
Whaddon folio *c.* 1460.

This boke late translate here in sight

By Antony Erle that vertuay knyght

Please it to accepte to youre noble grace

And at youre couenient leysoure and space

THE HOUSE OF YORK

1461-85

EDWARD IV 1461-83
RICHARD III 1483-5

Opposite: Edward IV with Elizabeth Woodville, the ill-fated Prince Edward
and his uncle Richard, Duke of Gloucester, later Richard III, from
The Dictes and Sayenges of the Phylosophers (*c.* 1477), the first dated book to be
printed in England.

EDWARD IV *r.* 1461-83

ORDS FAIL ME TO RELATE HOW well the commons love and adore him, as if he were their God. The entire kingdom keeps holiday for the event.' So wrote an Italian observer who witnessed the coronation of Edward IV on 28 June 1461.

The euphoria which greeted Edward is not difficult to understand. Over six feet tall and exceptionally good-looking, he had the physical presence of a king. At nineteen years of age he had already proved himself a brave and resourceful general. After the disaster of Wakefield which claimed the lives of his father, the Duke of York, his brother Edmund and his uncle, the Earl of Salisbury, he had defeated Jasper Tudor at Mortimer's Cross in Wales, saved London from Queen Margaret's northerners and won his crowning victory at Towton. With his prodigious feats on the battlefield he combined an instinctive grasp of political showmanship. He loved to be seen in public, dressed always in the latest fashions, and treated all his subjects, high and low, with the same easy familiarity. Among his many accomplishments was his reputation for being able to remember the names and fortunes of all his subjects of any importance throughout the kingdom.

He understood too the reasons why successive Parliaments under Henry IV and Henry VI had proved so stubborn in opposition to the sovereign. Edward won the approval of his Commons by adopting the policies once voiced in opposition. He saw it as his first priority to make the Crown solvent. The Crown lands were put in the hands of salaried officials rather than doled out at ludicrous rents to fortune-seeking courtiers and their clients. Many recipients of Lancastrian largesse found their lands confiscated or resumed by Act of Parliament. Detailed ordi-

Opposite: A portrait of Edward IV, who was considered exceptionally good looking and, at over six feet tall, had a kingly bearing which he displayed to full effect in the latest fashions.

The Seal of King Edward IV. The first ten years of Edward's reign were dominated by relations with his cousin, Richard Neville, Earl of Warwick, who, thanks to his immense influence, was tagged the 'Kingmaker'.

nances were set down for the control of the royal household expenses. The King also showed a keen interest in foreign trade and backed a number of successful commercial ventures as a merchant in his own right. Such measures testified not only to Edward's acumen but to the fact that the Yorkists owed a great deal of their support to the promise of better government and financial reform. Edward meant it when he told the Commons in 1467 that 'I purpose to live of mine own and not to charge my subjects but in great and urgent causes'.

However, these achievements really belong to the second part of Edward's reign. The first ten years were dominated by his relations with his power-hungry cousin, Richard Neville, Earl of Warwick. Although Edward wore the crown it was initially Warwick, fourteen years his senior, who called the tune. The Earl's pre-eminence was the supreme example of what inspired matchmaking could do for a family. Warwick's grandfather, Ralph Neville, had married Joan Beaufort, daughter of John of Gaunt. He could thus claim to be of royal blood as a great-great-grandson of Edward III. His father, also called Richard, acquired the earldom of Salisbury by marriage to the former Earl's daughter, Alice. This inheritance passed to Warwick when his father was captured and executed at Wakefield in 1460. Warwick himself married an even greater heiress, Anne Beauchamp, and through her acquired his earldom along with a vast inheritance in Wales and the West Midlands. His manors and castles spanned more than half the counties of England. Warwick's numerous brothers, sisters, uncles and aunts had also married well, none more so than his aunt Cicely Neville, a famed beauty who married the Duke of York and in April 1442 gave birth at Rouen to the future Edward IV.

Without the Neville connection the Yorkists could not have triumphed over the majority of the baronial houses who remained loyal to Henry VI. Warwick, a domineering, short-tempered and ambitious character, expected and received the rewards to match his services. He held office as Chamberlain of England, Captain of Calais and Warden of the Cinque Ports. The upbringing of Edward's youngest brother, Richard, was also entrusted to his care (at the ancestral Neville stronghold of Middleham in Yorkshire).

For the first four years of Edward's reign Warwick and his brother John continued their labours on the King's behalf. While they were mopping up the last pockets of Lancastrian resistance in the north, the King tasted the pleasures of court life at Westminster and Windsor. In 1464, after the decisive battle of Hexham, John Neville was rewarded with the hereditary Percy earldom of Northumberland and another brother, George Neville, became Archbishop of York.

But in the autumn of 1464 there arose the first signs of dissension between the great Earl and his royal cousin. Two issues – sex and diplomacy – appear to have been at the root of the trouble. Edward was an

ELIZABETH · VXOR
EDWARDVS · IIII

insatiable womaniser with, it appears, a special taste for older ladies. According to the contemporary French historian Philippe de Commynes, Edward 'thought upon nothing but women and that more than reason would'. Another foreigner, Dominic Mancini, who visited England towards the end of Edward's reign records that 'he pursued with no discrimination the married and the unmarried, the noble and lowly: however he took none by force. He overcame all by money and promises, and having conquered them, he dismissed them.' Early in the reign Edward apparently entered into a marriage contract with the widowed Lady Eleanor Butler, a daughter of old Talbot, 'the terror of the French', in order to coax her to his bed. In May 1464 another reluctant widow, Lady Elizabeth Woodville, refused to submit until Edward actually married her. With extraordinary lack of foresight the King agreed to her terms and the couple were secretly made man and wife, 'after which spousals ended, he went to bed and tarried there for four hours'.

At about the same time Warwick was negotiating with France's King Louis XI for a treaty of friendship which was to be sealed by the marriage of Edward IV to a French princess. These negotiations, which Warwick conducted off his own bat, meant a great deal to the Earl who was flattered by Louis's overtures and given to understand that he would receive French lands and titles as his reward. The revelation of Edward's secret marriage was therefore both a personal affront and a blow to Warwick's grandiose diplomatic ambitions. To rub salt in the wound the King's bride was the widow of a Lancastrian knight, and brought with her to court a swarm of relatives — two sons, five brothers and seven sisters — eager for advancement. Within two years of the marriage three of the sisters were in their turn married to the heirs of great baronial houses and one of her sons was married to the Duke of Exeter's daughter, previously pledged to a nephew of Warwick. The most notorious match was reserved for the Queen's brother, John: as one chronicler put it, 'Catherine, Duchess of Norfolk, a slip of a girl about eighty years old, was married to John Woodville, aged twenty years. A diabolical marriage.'

A Royal or rose noble struck during the reign of King Edward IV. He supported foreign trade and sponsored a number of successful commercial ventures as part of his plans for financial reform.

Opposite: The beautiful Lady Elizabeth Woodville, widow of a Lancastrian knight, withstood Edward's attentions until he married her, in secret, thereby spoiling the power-hungry Earl of Warwick's tactical negotiations for the King's marriage to a French princess.

Over the next four years (1464–8) Edward made it abundantly clear that he no longer regarded himself as Warwick's protégé. The King favoured an alliance with Burgundy, England's traditional ally and trading partner, and backed the proposal that his sister, Margaret, should marry Charles of Burgundy. At the same time he did not feel strong enough to put a stop to Warwick's flirtation with Louis VI. England's diplomacy thus had two masters, each pursuing contradictory aims while interested spectators, like Sir John Paston, placed bets on the outcome. In the spring of 1468 Edward had his way and Margaret married the Duke of Burgundy. This match tipped Warwick from sullen opposition into undeclared rebellion. He had made one King; why not another? A new puppet was ready in the wings in the shape of Edward's own brother, George, Duke of Clarence. The foolish Clarence nursed exalted notions of his own importance which the King did not apparently share. He had already aligned himself with Warwick over the Burgundian alliance and in 1467 Edward had to scotch his proposed marriage to Warwick's elder daughter, Isabel Neville. The prospect of a crown made Clarence an easy prey to the Kingmaker's new conspiracy.

It started early in 1469 with a series of Neville-inspired risings in the north and Midlands. In July Warwick and Clarence slipped across the Channel to Calais, where Clarence was married to Isabel. In the meantime Edward was bottled up at Nottingham, where he confronted a rebel army easily outnumbering his own. On 26 July 1469 a relief force coming to the King's aid was cut to pieces near Banbury. With disaster staring him in the face, Edward now decided on a strategic capitulation. He dispersed his army and allowed himself to fall into Warwick's hands.

This was a crucial gamble and it paid off. Warwick, who had intended to depose Edward with the assent of a compliant Parliament, found himself beset by a breakdown of local order reminiscent of the worst years of Henry VI's reign. The conspirators lost their nerve and far from deposing Edward they were compelled to release him so that order could be restored in the shires by the King's authority. The rebels were formally reconciled with their King and in October 1469 Edward returned to his capital. It was a brilliant recovery whereby military disaster was transformed into a political victory. However, it was abundantly clear that accounts would have to be settled. Edward could not contemplate a permanent truce with the man who had rebelled against him, executed the Queen's father and brother and turned his own brother against him. Warwick knew it too, and in the spring of 1470

Opposite: Statue of George, Duke of Clarence, the third son of Richard of York and brother of King Edward IV. During 1469–70 Warwick hoped to remove Edward and place Clarence on the throne. The plan failed and after Warwick's death in 1471 Edward's authority was unchallenged.

rebellion broke out again in Wales and in Lincolnshire at the Kingmaker's instigation. This time Edward put the rebels to flight, and Warwick, with the wretched Clarence still in tow, had to flee to France.

For Europe's master spinner of diplomatic webs, the 'universal spider' Louis XI, this was a god-sent opportunity. The once-mighty Earl of Warwick, so assiduously courted over the years, was now sufficiently humbled for Louis to pull off his cherished ambition: the reconciliation of the Kingmaker with Margaret of Anjou. On 22 July 1470 Warwick made his submission to Henry VI's Queen at Angers Cathedral. In September he was in England again accompanied by two Lancastrian stalwarts, the Earl of Oxford and Henry VI's half-brother, Jasper Tudor. Their landing caught Edward ill prepared in York; marching south he was very nearly captured by Warwick's brother, John. The King, accompanied by his brother, Richard of Gloucester, Lord Hastings and a few retainers, dashed across country to Lynn and embarked for Burgundy. While Warwick brought Henry VI out of the Tower and put him back on the throne, Edward's future lay in the hands of the Duke of Burgundy. Charles was at first reluctant to embroil himself in his brother-in-law's problems, but he changed his mind when first Louis XI and then Warwick declared war on him. He finally agreed to lend his brother-in-law a fleet and some 1,500 Burgundian troops, and on 11 March 1471 Edward set sail for the reconquest of his kingdom.

One month later the Kingmaker fought his last battle at Barnet. Apart from his superior generalship Edward owed his victory to the lingering suspicions between the old-guard Lancastrians and their new-found ally. Margaret of Anjou did not land in England until the very day of Warwick's defeat and death. On 4 May Edward caught up with her at Tewkesbury, and defeated her army as decisively as he had dealt with Warwick's. Thus Edward regained his crown and Louis forfeited, for the time being, his chance to swallow up the Duchy of Burgundy. As an added, if rather dubious, bonus Edward also recovered the allegiance of his brother Clarence, whose expectations of a crown had been quietly put aside when Warwick restored Henry VI. Henry himself fell victim to the power game in which he was no more than a befuddled bystander. On Edward's return to London from Tewkesbury, he was put to death in the Tower of London.

If the second half of Edward's reign lacks the drama and excitement of the first, it is because his authority remained unchallenged until his death. With the deaths of Warwick, Henry VI and his son Prince

Opposite: Parchment roll illuminated with historical passages from the life of Edward IV.

Edward, there was no need to proceed against the small fry. In contrast to the 113 Acts of Attainder passed on individuals after Towton in 1461, there were none after Barnet and Tewkesbury. Moreover the Queen, whom Edward had left behind in his precipitate flight to Burgundy, had now presented him with a son and the kingdom with an heir. In the twelve years left to him Edward was able at last to deliver the reforms that had been promised in the Yorkist manifestos of the 1450s. Contemporaries were greatly impressed by his efforts to suppress brigandage on the roads and prevent local magnates from taking the law into their own hands. The Crown was gradually freed from its burden of debt and Edward was able to make do for several years without asking Parliament for taxation measures.

There was one other aspect of the Yorkist programme which the King fully intended to carry out, and that was the reconquest of France. Louis XI had done his best to unseat Edward: now it was Edward's turn to try his luck against France. Edward's diplomacy during the years 1472–4 aimed at building up a grand alliance of Louis's enemies – the Duke of Brittany, the King of Aragon and, more crucial to its success, the Duke of Burgundy. In July 1475 Edward finally embarked for Calais with an army of 10,000 men, the largest and best-equipped host ever led into France by an English king, according to Commynes. Duke Charles, however, failed to meet his side of the bargain and arrived to meet his ally without any troops at all. He had left the Burgundian army far away at Nantes embroiled in another campaign on behalf of the Holy Roman Emperor. As Commynes again remarked, 'God had troubled his senses'. Deserted also by Francis, Duke of Brittany, and now confronted by Louis's formidable French army, Edward decided to abandon the whole enterprise in exchange for a hefty annual pension. On 29 August 1475 Louis and Edward met at Picquigny to seal the terms of a seven-year truce. The French entertained the entire English army at Amiens, after which Louis was heard to boast that he had evicted his would-be conquerors with venison pies and good wine.

The French peace provoked some grumbles of complaint in the English ranks, most notably from Edward's strait-laced brother, Richard of Gloucester. But it was the other brother, Clarence, who gave the King most cause for concern after his return to England. His unstable behaviour had long been a thorn in Edward's side. Although forgiven for his involvement with Warwick, Clarence had quarrelled with Richard of Gloucester over the division of Warwick's lands and breathed hints of

Opposite: From the memoirs of the contemporary French historian Philippe de Commynes, an illustration showing Edward IV landing at Calais in 1475 with an army of 10,000 men

saison. Et au regard de luy il
avoit son armee si rompue
si mal en point et si poure q̃l
ne losoit mostrer deuãt eulx /
Car il auoit perdu deuant
mez quatre mil homes pre
nans soulde / entre lesquelz
y mourut des meilleures gẽs
quil eust. Et ainsi verrez

de ce que son affaire reque
roit / et contre ce quil sca
noit et entendoit mieulx q̃
nul autre dix ans auoit.

Cõment le roy Edouard
dangleterre passa en france
et descendit a Calaix pour
faire la guerre au roy / et
de ce qui en aduint.

An illustration from *Des Proprietez des Choses* (see below), showing the dyeing of cloth.

treason when compelled to share the spoils. The crisis came in 1477 when Clarence, now a widower after Isabel's death in childbirth, wanted to marry the Duke of Burgundy's daughter, Mary. Edward refused point-blank to sanction this plan. Following her father's death in battle earlier in the year, Mary had become a great heiress and far too important a match for the unreliable Clarence. The enraged Clarence immediately plunged into fresh treasons. This time Edward had had enough. First a member of Clarence's household was accused of plotting the King's death by necromancy and executed; and when Clarence failed to heed the warning, he was arrested, attainted of treason in Parliament and sentenced to death. Egged on by the Queen, who had not forgotten Clarence's part in the death of her father and brother John in 1469, Edward permitted the sentence to be carried out on 18

Opposite: A depiction of miners at work taken from *Des Proprietez des Choses*, a nineteen-volume work by Jeandu Ries, which was specifically composed for Edward IV in 1482.

February 1478. Tradition has it that Clarence met his end in a butt of Malmsey wine and certainly his daughter, Margaret Pole, wore a model of a wine cock on her wrist in remembrance.

In reality Clarence was more of a nuisance than a threat. His execution was an unnecessary act of cruelty and points to the coarser side of Edward's nature. Three decades of warfare, treason and betrayal could not fail to leave their mark. It was an age of endemic violence which bred strange contradictions. Edward's former Constable, John Tiptoft, Earl of Worcester, who was executed during the Readeption of Henry VI is a good example; a widely travelled humanist scholar, he introduced with Edward's approval the practice of impalement for traitors and was nicknamed 'the butcher of England'.

Perhaps Edward's addiction to the pleasures of the flesh was another reaction to the temper of his age. 'In food and drink', wrote Mancini, 'he was most immoderate: it was his habit … to take an emetic for the delight of gorging his stomach once more. For this reason, and for the ease which was especially dear to him after his recovery of the Crown, he had grown fat in the loins.' Nor did he lose his taste for female company: towards the end of his life his particular favourite was the mercer's wife Jane Shore. 'For many he had, but her he loved,' wrote Sir Thomas More. In this curious blending of energy with laziness, ability with self-indulgence, Edward's character foreshadows that of his Tudor successor, Henry VIII.

In his leisure hours Edward also found time for artistic and cultural pursuits. He collected a fine library and spent considerable sums on the copying of manuscripts. During his Burgundian exile he was much taken with that recent invention, the printing press, and later became the friend and patron of William Caxton. In November 1477 Edward received from the Queen's brother, Anthony, Lord Rivers, a copy of

A page from Anthony Woodville's translation of *The Dictes and Sayenges of the Phylosophers*. William Caxton printed this work, the first printed book in England to bear a date, on his newly erected press in Westminster on 18 November 1477.

Prologue de lacteur sur la totalle recollation des sept volumes des an
chiennes et nouuelles cromques Dangleterre a la totale loenge du no
ble roy Edouard de ... ne de ce nom. Icta

Contemporary French illustration depicting Edward IV receiving a volume of the *Chronicle of England*. Edward was an ardent supporter of culture and the arts, collecting a fine library and financing the copying of manuscripts.

The Dictes and Sayenges of the Phylosophers, the first dated book to be printed in England.

During the last years of his reign, when war erupted again on the border with Scotland, Edward's robust constitution showed signs of giving way. In 1481 and again in 1482 elaborate plans to lead a great army north had to be postponed and the job was left to the King's able brother, Richard of Gloucester. In the winter of 1482–3 an even more ambitious project was mooted when Louis XI finally came to terms with Burgundy and cut off the annual payment to the English. Edward planned to invade France in person once again, and Parliament voted a generous subsidy. But it was too late. Edward contracted a fever and died on 9 April 1483. The Crown passed to his twelve-year-old heir, Prince Edward, and in his will the King appointed Richard of Gloucester as Protector.

RICHARD III *r.* 1483–5

K ING RICHARD REIGNED FOR ONLY two years and two months before he went down fighting at Bosworth Field. Nevertheless his reign has acquired an importance out of all proportion to its length. Richard was the last of thirteen kings of the Plantagenet line, which had ruled England since 1154. He was the last English King to die in battle. His death in 1485 is said to mark the boundary between the medieval and the modern ages. And he is the chief suspect in the longest and most emotive murder investigation in English history – the problem of who murdered the Princes in the Tower.

Richard's career also exemplifies the pitfalls confronting the biographer of any medieval figure. The records preserve the facts, but not the motives. In Richard's case no court history, no personal correspondence, not even a contemporary portrait survives to illumine his personality or his appearance. His image has been blackened in caricatures compiled in the reign of his successful rival, Henry VII, and later adapted by Shakespeare to give birth to the monster portrayed in his play *Richard III*.

Before seeking to untangle motives, it is therefore best to start with the unembroidered facts. Richard, fourth and last surviving son of Richard, Duke of York, and Cecily Neville, was born at Fotheringhay Castle in Northamptonshire on 2 October 1452. His childhood was soon affected by all the vicissitudes of the Wars of the Roses. When York and the Nevilles were put to flight at Ludlow in 1459 he and his brother George were placed in the custody first of the Duchess of Buckingham and then of the Archbishop of Canterbury. After York's death at Wakefield in December 1460 the Duchess of York took refuge with her

Opposite: Richard III, whose character and physical appearance are so linked in the public imagination to Shakespeare's demonic creation that it is hard to consider his reign objectively.

Ricus dns tercius dei gra Rex
anglie & Franc & dns hibnie

Dna Anna filia dni Comitis Warwici
dei gra Regina anglie & Franc & dna hib

two younger sons in the Burgundian Netherlands, where she remained until Edward's great victory at Towton made it safe to return. On the eve of Edward's coronation in June 1461 Richard, aged nine, became a Knight of the Garter and four months later the King created him Duke of Gloucester. For the best part of the next four years Richard's home was in the Yorkshire castle of Middleham, favourite residence of the Earl and Countess of Warwick. It was the custom among the nobility to farm out their children among families of equal rank, and, as the King's brother, Richard naturally rated the King's greatest subject. But when the great Earl's quarrel with Edward erupted into violence, Richard, unlike his brother George, remained steadfastly loyal to the King. In 1469 he was appointed Constable of England and charged with the suppression of a rising in Wales.

Richard's apprenticeship was now at an end: from 1469 till Edward's death Richard was to play a key role, both military and administrative, in the affairs of the kingdom. In 1470 he accompanied Edward in his flight to Burgundy, while the Warwick–Lancaster alliance restored Henry VI to his throne. At the battles of Barnet and Tewkesbury in 1471 Richard commanded with distinction a wing of the Yorkist army. There is no foundation for later stories that Richard was present at, or took part in, the death of Henry VI's son, Prince Edward. Contemporary accounts simply state that Edward was killed during the battle. He was probably present at the Tower on the night Henry himself was put to death, but so were many other Yorkist leaders.

With the Yorkists safely restored to power, Richard was chosen to take up Warwick's former task of pacifying the lawless northern counties and sealing the border against Scottish incursions. This commission was to keep Richard occupied intermittently until 1475 and almost exclusively thereafter. In the autumn of 1471 Richard married Anne Neville, the sixteen-year-old widow of Prince Edward and younger daughter of the Kingmaker. As co-heiress of the Beauchamp estate, which Warwick had held in his wife's right, Anne brought her husband a valuable inheritance; but there is reason to suppose that Richard's intentions were not exclusively mercenary. He had grown up with Anne during his stay at Middleham, and subsequently treated her mother with kindness and generosity. This much cannot be said for George, Duke of Clarence, the husband of Warwick's other daughter, Isabel. George was in fact so keen to keep his hands on the whole of the Countess's estates that he put every obstacle in the way of Richard's marriage, including the attempted

Opposite: The figure on the right is Anne Neville, the younger daughter of Warwick the Kingmaker. She was initially married to Prince Edward, son of Henry VI, but after his death married Richard, Duke of Gloucester, in 1741.

abduction of the intended bride. With Edward's mediation it was agreed that the marriage should go ahead, but that most of the Beauchamp estates would be reserved for Clarence. Early in 1473 Anne bore Richard a son, whom they christened Edward. Though he fathered at least two bastards before his marriage, he was faithful to her afterwards.

In 1475 Richard took part in the inglorious but profitable French campaign that ended with the Treaty of Picquigny. We are told that the Duke of Gloucester opposed this betrayal of the Agincourt spirit and so earned the distrust of France's King Louis XI.

The last act in Clarence's pitiful career provided the occasion for Richard's next visit to court in the autumn of 1477. Continually threatened by the disloyalty of Clarence, Edward at last had him tried for high treason. Despite the earlier rancour over the Warwick–Beauchamp inheritance Richard was, according to one contemporary account, 'overcome with grief for his brother' when the death sentence was carried out. Three days after Clarence had been drowned in a wine butt the Duke of Gloucester procured a licence to set up two religious foundations to pray for his dead brother and other members of the royal family. Our source, the level-headed Italian cleric Dominic Mancini, goes on to say that 'thenceforth Richard came very rarely to court. He kept himself within his own lands and set out to acquire the loyalty of his people through favours and justice. The good reputation of his private life and public activities powerfully attracted the esteem of strangers … Such was his renown in warfare, that whenever a difficult and dangerous policy had to be undertaken, it would be entrusted to his discretion and generalship. By these arts Richard acquired the favour of the people, and avoided the jealousy of the Queen, from whom he lived far separated.'

Clearly there was no love lost between Richard and his sister-in-law, the Woodville Queen. Like many of the aristocracy he probably resented the favour shown to her innumerable relatives, and it is possible that he also held her responsible for Clarence's death. In any event he preferred a life of service in the north to the intrigues and luxury of Edward's court. Nor is there any doubt that his lieutenancy in the north merited Mancini's complimentary remarks. The records of the City of York contain many references to his activities – from suppressing illegal fish traps to commuting taxes in times of need – and record the gratitude of the city fathers: 'The Duke of Gloucester shall, for his great labour … be presented … with six swans and six pikes.' His legal commissions also toured the West Riding, Cumberland and Westmorland

Opposite: The Rous Roll, showing the proper heraldic devices for Richard III, Anne Neville and their son Prince Edward, who died before his father's death at Bosworth Field in 1485.

IACOBVS 3 D GRATIA
REX SOTORVM

dispensing 'good and indifferent [i.e. impartial] justice to all who sought it, were they rich or poor, gentle or simple'.

As Warden of the West March Richard was also responsible for the defence of the border country, and from 1480 conducted several hard-fought campaigns against King Louis's ally, James III of Scotland. These culminated in 1482 with the recapture of Berwick and an unopposed entry into Edinburgh. Edward's gratitude for this victory and the ten solid years of service preceding it was expressed in 1483 when Parliament made the Duke of Gloucester's Wardenship of the West March a hereditary office and granted him all the royal manors and revenues in the county of Cumberland. This palatinate state within a state which Richard now controlled was a fitting reward for a brother who had more than fulfilled the promise of his adopted motto, 'Loyaulté Me Lie', loyalty binds me. Parliament approved the grant in February: two months later Edward IV died.

So passed the first thirty years of Richard's thirty-three years. Had he, rather than Edward, died in 1483 he would no doubt have earned a respectable footnote in history as an able soldier, a conscientious administrator and a self-effacingly loyal brother; a man whose old-fashioned sense of honour led him to disapprove of Picquigny-style diplomacy as much as the free-wheeling sexual mores of Edward's court; a blameless husband who remained faithful to his wife and shielded her relatives from the consequences of Warwick's fall. And yet, within six months of his brother's death he had bastardised Edward's children, executed Edward's closest friend, seized the Crown for himself and driven Edward's Queen into an improbable alliance with an obscure Lancastrian pretender named Henry Tudor.

Events came quickly to a head after Edward IV's death on 9 April 1483. The Woodville clan, led by the Queen, knew that they had many enemies including Richard of Gloucester whom Edward had named Protector in his will. They therefore opted for attack as the best means of defence. While Richard was still in the north they passed a resolution through the Council to replace Gloucester's protectorship with a regency council. They also arranged for the young Edward V to be brought from Ludlow to London as quickly as possible for his coronation. Once he was crowned the protectorship would lapse in any case. Clearly the Woodvilles were aware from the start that Richard might opt to grab the throne for himself. As Mancini says, 'they were afraid that if Richard took the crown, or even governed alone, they who bore

Opposite: James III King of Scotland and ally of Louis XI of France. Richard fought several campaigns against James culminating in a triumphant entry into Edinburgh in 1482.

the blame of Clarence's death would suffer death or at least be ejected from their high estate'.

Lord Hastings, an intimate friend of the late King, but no lover of the Queen's affinity, let slip these plans to Richard. With the help of another Woodville opponent, the powerful Duke of Buckingham, Richard promptly intercepted Edward v on the road to London and arrested his guardian, Anthony Woodville, Earl Rivers. When the news reached London on 1 May, the Queen immediately took sanctuary at Westminster with her younger son, Richard. The Dukes of Gloucester and Buckingham entered London unopposed on 4 May.

It is not strictly relevant to ask who was the aggressor in this situation, for the answer is that each party acted in self-defence for fear of the other. The situation itself was a legacy of Edward iv's marriage, which created the rift between the Woodvilles and the older aristocracy. Richard came out on top because the Woodvilles, without Edward's protection, were no match for their enemies. However, the Protector's position was still decidedly tricky. At the age of twelve his nephew was by contemporary standards nearly an adult, and his coronation could not be indefinitely postponed. Preparations were in fact going ahead for the coronation to take place on 24 June. Once deprived of his authority as Protector Richard could not expect Edward v to side with him against the boy's own mother and his former guardian. The logical conclusion was simple enough: to survive Richard must rule, and to rule he must be King.

By the second week of June Richard had decided to make his pitch for the throne. His faithful Yorkshiremen were summoned to 'come unto us to London … with as many as ye can make defensibly arrayed, there to aid and assist us against the Queen, her bloody adherents and affinity'. On 16 June Prince Richard was removed from Westminster Sanctuary with threats of force and joined his elder brother in the Tower. All this was done under the pretext that the Queen's 'bloody adherents' were hatching a murderous plot, but in the meantime Richard was sounding out his principal supporters on the idea that he should be crowned in place of his nephew. Buckingham, a headstrong man with a special grudge against the Woodvilles, was willing enough; but some of the old guard from Edward iv's reign, notably Lord Hastings, would not stomach the disinheritance of Edward's children. Without hesitation Richard had him arrested at a Council meeting and beheaded on the spot. Two days later, on 22

June, the Lord Mayor's brother, Dr Ralph Shaw, preached a sermon at Paul's Cross on the text 'bastard slips shall not take deep root': his message was that Edward IV had made a marriage contract with Lady Eleanor Butler before his subsequent marriage to Elizabeth Woodville. Under canon law this would have invalidated the Woodville marriage and made bastards of their children. The true heir to the throne was therefore none other than the Duke of Gloucester. At the end of June Parliament met and assented to a document petitioning Richard to take the throne. The petition was brought to Richard at Baynard's Castle, where he graciously accepted after a show of reluctance. Richard's coronation on 6 July was attended by virtually the entire peerage, including Henry Tudor's mother, Margaret Beaufort.

Despite the exemplary speed and efficiency with which Richard carried out his *coup d'état*, he was soon prey to the same sort of troubles as the Lancastrian usurper Henry IV had encountered some eighty years earlier. He was on a royal progress at Lincoln in October 1483 when he learned that his chief accomplice, Buckingham, was now in arms against him, having come to terms both with the Woodvilles and with the exiled Henry Tudor. Buckingham's revolt seems as gratuitous as that of the Percys in 1403: according to Henry VII's historian, Polydore Vergil, Buckingham had encouraged Richard's usurpation simply as the stepping stone to his own elevation. Whatever the motives behind it, the whole carefully co-ordinated rebellion ended in fiasco. After heavy rainstorms melted his army, the Duke was taken without a battle and executed on 2 November at Salisbury. Henry Tudor's little invasion fleet turned back to Brittany without attempting a landing and Richard's able lieutenant, the Duke of Norfolk, dispersed scattered risings in the south-east.

Richard had won the first round; but the revolt had crystallised the pattern of opposition to his rule and left little doubt that a second round would follow. Elizabeth Woodville, by now convinced that she would never see her sons alive again, had made an agreement with Henry Tudor that he would marry her eldest daughter, also named Elizabeth. Since Henry was the sole surviving heir to the Lancastrian claim and Elizabeth was the eldest daughter of Edward IV, this alliance was just as dangerous as the earlier *rapprochement* between Warwick and Margaret of Anjou. The Wars of the Roses created some strange bedfellows.

For Richard 1484 was a year of watching and waiting for the expected invasion. It was also witness to a personal tragedy and a diplomatic failure both of which seriously undermined his position. In April his only son, Prince Edward, died at Middleham. In the words of one chronicler, 'you might have seen his father and mother in a state almost bordering on madness by reason of their sudden grief'. Without a direct heir Richard was a far less likely prospect to the many who had tacitly supported his coup in the hope of avoiding a trouble-ridden minority. In the summer the King narrowly failed in his attempt to extradite Henry Tudor from Brittany. Henry escaped and found refuge at the court of a far more powerful friend, King Charles VIII of France. The year ended with only one success, a three-year truce with the Scots, which was sealed with great solemnity at Nottingham Castle in September. At Christmas the King learned from his agents in France that the invasion was definitely scheduled for the following summer.

The campaigning season of 1485 opened with a propaganda war. The death of Queen Anne in March – another blow to the beleaguered King – gave rise to rumours that he had poisoned her in order to marry Henry Tudor's intended bride, Elizabeth of York. It was not until 7 August that the Tudor made his landing at Milford Haven in South Wales. The final battle took place on Monday 22 August a few miles west of Leicester, near the village of Market Bosworth. Anxious as ever to settle the affair by direct action, Richard led a cavalry charge directed at the person of his rival and was slain in the mêlée. The Earl of Northumberland, who led Richard's rearguard, watched the proceedings as a spectator, while the Stanley brothers threw their levies into battle on Henry's side. When it was over Richard's naked body was strung over the back of a pack-horse and taken to Leicester for burial in the Grey Friars' chapel.

It seems likely that the country as a whole shared the Earl of Northumberland's view of the conflict. It mattered little who won at Bosworth because the issue at stake was simply a dynastic one. Even the dynastic issue was confused by the split within the Yorkist camp and the promised marriage of the Lancastrian Henry to Elizabeth of York. In the earlier stages of the Wars of the Roses, when the Yorkists promised good government in place of Lancastrian incompetence and corruption, there had been real issues to fight over. In 1485 it came to a choice between a childless usurper and a little-known Welshman who had spent most of his life in exile. Richard's only mourners were the knights and squires of his personal following – many of whom fell at his side – and those who remembered his administration in the north: 'King

Opposite: Richard III with his fool, from an illuminated manuscript of music made for the court. Jesters were a feature of court life until the seventeenth century.

et siu · ps · Benedictus

dominus. Omnes fines terre.

sunt in iniquitatibz : non est
nis de celo prospexit sup filio
h̄ est intelligens aut requirens
dimanetunt simul inutiles fac
fatat boni non est usque ad un
omnes qui operant iniquitate

A wood carving depicting the head of Richard III, the last English King to die on the field of battle. Richard died at Bosworth Field on 22 August 1485.

Richard, late mercifully reigning upon us, was … piteously slain and murdered, to the great heaviness of this city.' A brave tribute from the civic records of York.

Richard's career is too often judged on the issue of whether or not he had the Princes in the Tower murdered. The evidence is not conclusive, but it seems highly probable that he did. The Princes were not seen alive after the autumn of 1483 and Mancini feared they might already be dead when he left the country at the end of June. Had they still been living in 1484 or 1485 Richard would surely have produced them to scupper Henry Tudor's marriage plans. The murder of two innocent children was a horrible crime even by fifteenth-century standards, but it is difficult to see how Richard could have let them live without risking needless conspiracies in their names.

Richard's real failing as a king was his inability to win over the great magnates whose support was crucial to any medieval regime. For all his solid virtues as an administrator and his undoubted courage in battle, Richard lacked Edward IV's knack of making friends and he was a bad judge of character. He allowed Buckingham to lead him by the nose, and made an enemy of his erstwhile supporter, Lord Hastings. The Earl of Northumberland was his close associate in the north for ten years, but not, it seems, his friend. Lord Stanley was close at Richard's side for two years but turned his coat at the vital moment. Louis XI found him unsympathetic, and Sir Thomas More, admittedly a biased witness, described Richard's nature as 'close and secret'. Ill at ease with his peers, Richard preferred to put his trust in boyhood friends or able lieutenants who owed their positions to his favour. Three of these, William Catesby, Sir Richard Ratcliffe and Francis Lovell, are unflatteringly commemorated in the famous doggerel verse:

> *The Cat, the Rat*
> *And Lovell our Dog*
> *Rulen all England*
> *Under an Hog.*

Yet it was clearly a military rather than a political verdict that settled Richard's fate. Bosworth was the supreme test of his right to rule, just as Shrewsbury was for Henry IV, Towton for Henry VI, and Barnet and Tewkesbury for Edward IV. Richard failed and the crown, reputedly retrieved on the battlefield from under a gorse bush, was placed by Lord Stanley on the head of the first Tudor King.

INDEX

PICTURE CREDITS

Weidenfeld & Nicolson Archives: endpapers, pages 2, 19, 30, 36, 38, 39, 40, 47, 55, 62, 86, 90, 99
The Bridgeman Art Library, London: pages 12, 24, 27, 28, 31, 37, 41, 42, 45, 46, 50, 53, 56, 61,
63, 64, 70, 74, 76, 79, 80, 83, 84, 85, 89, 94, 100
AKG London: pages 15, 20, 87
theartarchive: pages 23, 32, 34–35, 48–49, 54, 67, 68, 77, 93
By permission of the Warden and Fellows of New College, Oxford: page 51
Topham Picturepoint: pages 59, 73